W9-BMV-786

When modern business-management theories collide with wisdom from the Bible, leader reputations feel the impact. Jim Seybert challenges and encourages you to wisely lead your enterprise *and* demonstrate your relationship with Christ to your employees, customers, and vendors.
—**PAUL MARTIN**, president of Advocace Media, LLC

With creative perspectives on well-known biblical stories and principles of leadership and marketing, this book lets you experience what Jim Seybert does for his clients: You get a different vision of your organization, your leadership, the world you seek to serve, and the future God has for you. Your leadership abilities, your time to lead, and the lives of those who follow you are priceless gifts that God has entrusted to you. *Leadership RE:Vision* gives you the insights and the practical action steps you can take to lead well in the Kingdom work God has given you.
—**RICHARD KRIEGBAUM**, author of *Leadership Prayers*

In *Leadership RE:Vision*, Jim Seybert challenges conventional leadership thinking, sets a fresh context for leaders' actions, and calls for a new direction of principled leadership!
—**BOB BROWER, PHD**, president of Point Loma Nazarene University, San Diego, California

To say this book is a breath of fresh air is an incalculable understatement. Jim's message is for leaders of all ages, in all stages of life, with all levels of experience.

I have come into contact with a considerable number of leadership books. Many I have given away, some I have kept and read carefully, and a few I have read over and over. I will do all three with this book, and it will become required reading for my executive MBAs.
—**DR. TOM A. BUCKLES**, professor of marketing at Biola University

Jim puts his leadership lenses on, dives into the Bible, and helps us refocus our vision around leadership that blesses people. I read what I endorse, and I really enjoyed Jim's work, especially his key insights into the biblical narrative.
—**REGGIE MCNEAL**, leadership consultant and author of *The Present Future*

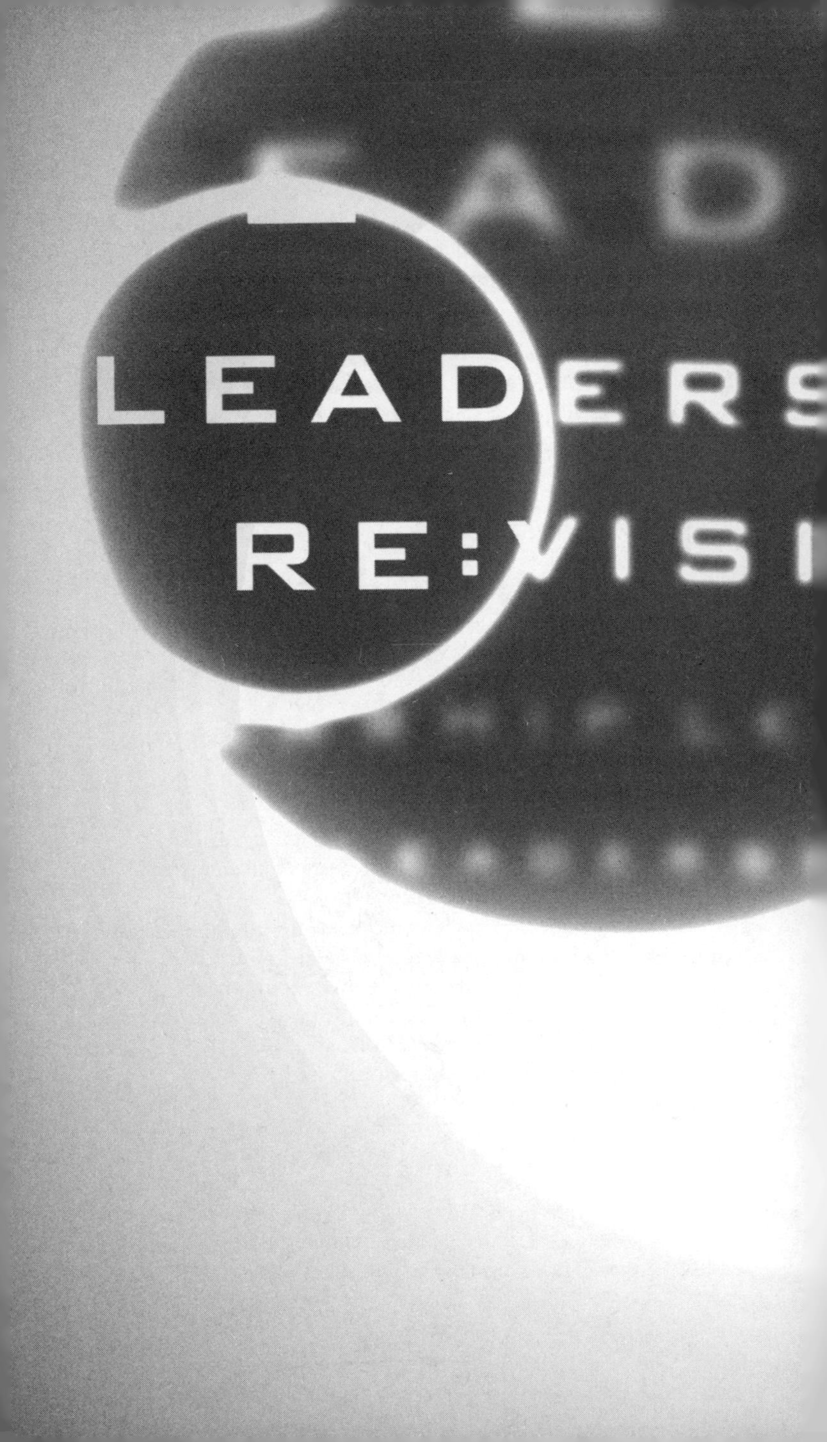
LEADERS
RE:VISI

JIM SEYBERT

Tyndale House Publishers, Inc. Carol Stream, Illinois

Visit Tyndale's exciting Web site at www.tyndale.com

Visit Jim's Web site at www.jimseybert.com

TYNDALE and Tyndale's quill logo are registered trademarks of Tyndale House Publishers, Inc.

Leadership RE:Vision

Copyright © 2009 by Jim Seybert. All rights reserved.

Cover photo copyright © by Veer. All rights reserved.

Cover image of wood grain copyright © by Creatas/Jupiter Images. All rights reserved.

Author photo copyright © by Amy Wellenkamp, www.amywellenkamp.com. All rights reserved.

Designed by Erik M. Peterson

Edited by Susan Taylor

Published in association with the literary agency of Mark Sweeney & Associates, Bonita Springs, Florida 34135

The author's discussion of the differences between checkers and chess was adapted from Irving Chernev, *Wonders and Curiosities of Chess* (Dover Publications, 1975).

Unless otherwise indicated, all Scripture quotations are taken from the *Holy Bible,* New Living Translation, copyright © 1996, 2004, 2007 by Tyndale House Foundation. (Some quotations may be from the NLT, first edition, copyright © 1996.) Used by permission of Tyndale House Publishers, Inc., Carol Stream, Illinois 60188. All rights reserved.

Scripture quotations marked KJV are taken from *The Holy Bible*, King James Version.

Library of Congress Cataloging-in-Publication Data

Seybert, Jim.
  Leadership RE:vision / Jim Seybert.
    p. cm.
  Includes index.
  ISBN-13: 978-1-4143-2225-4 (sc)
  ISBN-10: 1-4143-2225-9 (sc)
  1. Leadership—Religious aspects—Christianity. I. Title.
  BV4597.53.L43S49 2009
  253—dc22
                                        2008034384

Printed in the United States of America

15 14 13 12 11 10 09
7   6   5   4   3   2   1

Dedicated to the memory
of my grandmother Juana Coon,
who waited patiently for me to finish
writing before going home.

CONTENTS

INTRODUCTION

I GOT MY FIRST SET OF EYEGLASSES WHEN I was in the seventh grade. I still remember walking out of the doctor's office and saying to my mom, "Wow, I can actually see the leaves on those trees."

I didn't know how bad my eyes were, so I hadn't been worried about not seeing the leafy detail. The thought that I was missing something never crossed my mind because it was outside my scope of experience and understanding. The new glasses—big dorky brown plastic frames and all—provided a revised perspective. They helped me see things I had never seen—had never even considered seeing—before.

My hope is that this little book can become that new pair of glasses for you.

Leadership RE:Vision isn't about changing your goals or objectives. It's about challenging the conventional wisdom and long-held premises of what it means to be a leader. It's about looking at your leadership habits from a new perspective and using a different set of standards to measure the success of your efforts.

- Are you too patient with people who waste your time? *Leadership RE:Vision* will help you see the value of ignoring them.

- Are you trying hard to be a selfless leader? *Leadership RE:Vision* will encourage you to celebrate the *self* God intended you to be.
- Has a lack of experience held you back from stepping up and really leading? *Leadership RE:Vision* will suggest that past success can be a slippery slope to failure.

I intend to rattle your assumptions and challenge the status quo, but these aren't new ideas. In fact, the foundations for *Leadership RE:Vision* are as old as time itself. The Bible is packed with lessons on leadership. God filled the pages of his book with examples of leaders—good and bad. Somewhere along the line, our ideas of what it means to be an effective leader have been tweaked and disjointed into a style that is out of kilter with what I think God intended.

Leadership RE:Vision is my attempt to help you put on a new set of glasses and to really see the leaves.

—Jim Seybert

DON'T WASTE GOD'S TIME

A group of men whose hearts God had touched went with [Saul]. But there were some scoundrels who complained, "How can this man save us?" And they scorned him and refused to bring him gifts. But Saul ignored them.

1 SAMUEL 10:26-27

ONE OF MY FAVORITE LEADERSHIP STORIES from the Bible happened when Saul was the newly appointed first king of Israel.

Saul had a mission to accomplish—God's mission. He was the person chosen to lead God's people. This was the next step in God's strategic plan to fulfill his promise to Abram that he would make Abram's descendants into a great nation and that through him "all the families on earth" would be blessed (Genesis 12:3).

The people of Israel had never been at this place. They'd never had a king. The status quo was changing. God didn't choose Saul to manage the people; he chose Saul to lead them.

Saul had a group of men around him who

were dialed into the mission. They weren't supporting Saul the man so much as they were supporting the mission he represented. These advisers certainly didn't agree with everything Saul suggested. (Counselors are worthless if they're merely yes-men.) But God had touched their hearts, and they provided Saul with valuable input as he began his reign as Israel's first king. They understood what Saul was trying to do, and they gave him advice.

COUNSELORS ARE WORTHLESS IF THEY'RE MERELY YES-MEN.

But there was a group of people who just wanted to get in the way. These naysayers didn't just have a different idea about how or why to *move forward*; their purpose—if indeed they even had a purpose—was to stop progress dead in its tracks.

LEADERS LEAD

If you've spent any time in a leadership role, you know about such people. You may even be thinking of some of them right now and could name them if I asked you to.

They ask the same questions and raise the same tired old flags at every meeting. They push personal agendas that are counter to the group's mission and goals. Even after decisions have been made and the organization is poised to move ahead, these "scoundrels" (God's description) stand in the way and impede forward momentum.

You might think Saul would try to negotiate a solution or find a way to compromise. But he doesn't. He doesn't try to reason with these men. He doesn't change course to accommodate them. What *does* Saul do when these men get in the way? He ignores them. One Bible translation says he turned a deaf ear to them.

Turn a Deaf Ear

When I was a kid, we had a family friend who had 100 percent hearing loss. Ben was, as he described it, "deaf as a fence post." Ben read lips amazingly well. His eyes had become his ears, and if he could see you, he could "hear" what you were saying.

Ben and his wife clearly shared a deep love for each other, but they were also world-class arguers. When they argued, Ben would stare intently at his wife's lips to hear what she was saying. They'd go on for great lengths, but when Ben was finished with the conversation, he would put up his hand and squeeze his eyes tightly shut. If he couldn't see, he couldn't hear. When Ben closed his eyes, the world around him ceased to exist.

Saul was God's appointed leader, and when a mission-busting group of scoundrels tried to steer him off course, Saul treated them as if he couldn't hear them, as if they didn't even exist. And here's the clincher: There's no evidence that God punished Saul for this behavior. In fact, there's good reason to believe that eventually listening to these people is what got Saul into hot water with God.

LEADERSHIP RE:VISION

It's easy to confuse leadership and management. A manager's task is to maintain the status quo, follow established procedures, and evaluate performance based on accepted standards. Some managers are also leaders, and some leaders do a good job of managing. The two functions are often interchanged and combined, but they are not the same.

As the leader, you're the one who stands at the door and says, "Come and look outside. I've seen what's out there, and it's awesome," or "I know the policy manual says to follow *this* procedure, but I think we need to try something different."

Conventional wisdom suggests that effective leadership requires an open-door policy in which all complaints are heard and considered. But I don't see that described in Scripture. The apostle Paul says that people who are causing divisions aren't worth a third hearing (see Titus 3:10), and when it comes to people who have ulterior motives, he accuses the Corinthian believers of finding pleasure in "putting up with fools" (see 2 Corinthians 11:19-20).

God is above time. He exists outside of time. He created it and has an endless supply of it. Yet even God shows us that he won't waste time on those who refuse to get with the program. Scripture is full of examples where in one way or another God says enough is enough.

SCRIPTURE IS FULL OF EXAMPLES WHERE GOD SAYS ENOUGH IS ENOUGH.

If the One who has an endless supply of time draws a line in the sand, why are you allowing those people whose names you thought of just a few paragraphs ago to derail the mission you have to accomplish with your limited amount of time?

The next time you are facing a situation where these folks will have an opportunity to disrupt a meeting with their predictable behavior, take them aside beforehand and let them know that you will no longer tolerate their attempts to derail forward progress. Give them a chance to ask their questions in private, answer them to the best of your ability, and warn them that there is nothing to be gained by asking the same questions again.

Be gracious and speak lovingly, but don't give in to their agendas.

Do whatever you do in the name of the Lord. He's given you a job to do and a finite amount of time to do it. Don't let the scoundrels trip you up.

2

CUSTOMERS DON'T ALWAYS COME FIRST

Even when I walk through the darkest valley, I will not be afraid, for you are close beside me. Your rod and your staff protect and comfort me. You prepare a feast for me in the presence of my enemies.

PSALM 23:4-5

THE IMAGE OF A SHEPHERD AND HIS SHEEP is one of the most prevalent in Scripture. References to sheep are woven into many significant biblical story arcs because the sheep-and-shepherd relationship is such a good image for the way God intends us to live.

There will always be those who lead and those who follow. Those who lead one day will follow someone else the next. Shepherds will always be charged with protecting their sheep. Sheep will always need someone to lead and protect them. Neither is more important than the other. Shepherds need sheep. Without a flock, they'd wander around the hills looking for something to do. Sheep need a shepherd to provide protection and keep the flock moving in the same direction.

It makes sense for shepherds to take care of their sheep, just as the flock's best interest lies in following the shepherd's lead. It's a symbiotic arrangement. It just works.

David paints an incredible picture with the words of Psalm 23. He clearly has a deep knowledge of the sheep-and-shepherd dynamic, having been a shepherd before he succeeded Saul as king. But he must have also had a strong sense of his role as a member of God's flock. He knew what it was like to be a sheep. How else could he have so touchingly written from a sheep's perspective?

Most commentaries on Psalm 23 focus on the sheep's need to accept the shepherd's loving protection. If we obey and follow our Shepherd, he will lead us beside peaceful streams. He is the Good Shepherd and leaves us wanting for nothing.

YOUR ROLE AS A LEADER IS TO LEAD YOUR FLOCK BESIDE QUIET WATERS.

Now look at David's poetry though the shepherd's eyes. Your role as a leader is to provide for and protect your flock, renew their strength, lead them beside quiet waters, and fill their cups to overflowing. God does this for his sheep, and we should emulate God's leadership examples.

Carla was the quintessential customer-service rep. She greeted every call with a warm smile and went the extra mile to solve problems. She had the ultimate servant's heart. You could often hear her praying before a call, asking God to help her provide great service to those she considered to be in her "flock." You could count on Carla to brighten your day, and customers from all across the country frequently commented on her wonderful spirit.

9

But that spirit was consumed in a raging fire whenever one particular customer called. This individual was so spiteful that Carla was often in tears before the end of the call.

The customer accused Carla of mistakes she hadn't made, making his own habitual inability to meet deadlines somehow her fault. He demanded special treatment when he made careless mistakes, expected refunds when he changed his mind midstream, and generally treated Carla as if she were his personal punching bag.

Carla repeatedly asked, and then begged, her supervisor for relief. In true servant fashion, she didn't want the customer turned over to another customer-service rep. She just wanted her boss to "please talk to him and find out what I can do to help him." But her boss, her shepherd, refused to challenge the guy because "the customer is always right."

In the mind of her boss, this mean-spirited customer's behavior had to be tolerated, no matter how harmful it was to Carla. Customers pay the bills, and poor treatment comes with the territory when you are a service rep. But Paul encourages us to avoid copying the behavior and customs of this world (see Romans 12:2). If Carla's boss had looked at himself as a good shepherd, I doubt he would have tolerated such boorish disregard for one of his sheep.

Unfortunately, Carla was never granted relief. Feeling betrayed and totally drained, she left the company. That was a tremendous loss for her, for the company, and for all the other decent customers who depended on her to take care of their needs.

LEADERSHIP RE:VISION

My purpose in writing this book is to help you think differently about the way you lead. My hope is that as you read these pages, you'll be challenged to think about your leadership approach and consider making some changes in those places where you sense God nudging you.

How would you have handled the customer who mistreated Carla? *Is* the customer always right?

We've been fed that line for so long that we tend to accept it at face value, no questions asked. But do we really believe it? Should one unreasonable customer be allowed to adversely affect our ability to serve everyone else? Which relationship is more important in God's eyes—the one you have with your customer or the one you have with your employee?

Do the behaviors and customs of this world dictate that we abdicate our roles as shepherds, or are we called to lead with a different set of standards? Are you using your rod and your staff to comfort the sheep God has placed under your care?

3

GOOD STEWARDSHIP DOESN'T MEAN STINGINESS

[Jesus said,] "You know that the rulers in this world lord it over their people, and officials flaunt their authority over those under them. But among you it will be different."

MATTHEW 20:25-26

WHEN DID BEING A GOOD STEWARD BECOME synonymous with being cheap? If there's anywhere that Christian leaders need to step away from traditional values and cut a new path, it's right here. I've heard otherwise-wonderful Christian leaders discuss wage-and-benefit issues as if their employees were out to rip them off for every cent they had.

When some of Jesus' disciples griped because two of their own had requested special treatment, Jesus rebuked them. The world does things a certain way, he said, but "among you it will be different" (Matthew 20:26). Jesus was calling his followers to treat those who follow them in a fashion unlike conventional wisdom suggested they should. He was encouraging them—and us—to establish and operate by different standards.

Despite this, far too many Christian leaders regularly march in lockstep with their nonbelieving colleagues. Instead of being magnanimous, they are miserly. To put it bluntly, when it comes to salaries, wages, and benefits, many Christian organizations and Christian business leaders are less than fair.

Jesus promised his followers abundant life. And while he wasn't referring to people's paychecks when he made that promise, having a decent salary certainly doesn't hurt. Are you contributing to the "abundance" of the people who look to you for their livelihood?

God takes very seriously the idea of treating workers fairly. In Malachi 3:5 he lists those who cheat their employees in the same verse as sorcerers, adulterers, and liars. He says he will speak against those who cheat their workers. James writes, "The wages you held back [from your workers] cry out against you" (5:4).

Cheating is nothing more than operating in a way that gives one an unfair or undeserved advantage, and only the most vile of employers would admit to purposely cheating their workers. But take a minute to consider the following scenarios: Are employees being cheated when

- managers repeatedly fail to conduct scheduled salary and performance reviews and delay potential salary adjustments?
- employers withhold scheduled raises until employees come and ask for what was promised?
- top managers are paid ten, twenty, or even one hundred times more than hourly workers?
- three people are now required to do the work of five because of painful staff reductions?
- worthy employees are denied deserved raises because the job market is tight and they can't afford to leave and seek work elsewhere?

LEADERS LEAD

Being different doesn't mean being foolish. Jesus did not say, "Among you there will be some very unwise practices." The issue is more about your attitude and approach to compensation than about the actual dollars. Paying people more than their work is worth or more than you can afford is not good for the long-term fiscal health of your organization, and God wants you to succeed in the task he's given you. But perhaps it's time to consider setting some new compensation standards in your organization.

When you think about wages for employees, do you tend to pay them as much as you can afford to pay or as little as they'll agree to? Think about God's generosity toward you. Are you imitating him when it comes to paying your staff?

Charles Dickens's immortal curmudgeon, Ebenezer Scrooge, is remembered for the turnabout he exhibited after being visited by three spirits. During his visit to Christmas Past, he looks on as his former employer, Mr. Fezziwig, prepares for a party on Christmas Eve. The spirit expresses to Scrooge a sense of wonder at how much happiness Fezziwig is able to bring his employees with "but a few pounds of your mortal money."

Scrooge responds, "He has the power to render us happy or unhappy; to make our service light or burdensome; a pleasure or a toil. Say that his power lies in words and looks; in things so slight and insignificant that it is impossible to add and count 'em up: what then? The happiness he gives is quite as great as if it cost a fortune."

LEADERSHIP RE:VISION

It's time for Christians in leadership positions to examine their attitudes toward wages from a new perspective. Followers of Christ should operate in the world but avoid conformity to the world's lower standards. Too many of us look the other way when we're confronted with biblical directives to follow God's example of generosity.

As an advocate for change in this area, I have participated in many executive sessions involving the discussion of wages and have heard otherwise godly men and women dismiss scriptural imperatives not to cheat workers with excuses that sound something like this: "I know what the Bible says, but this is business."

FOLLOWERS OF CHRIST SHOULD OPERATE IN THE WORLD BUT AVOID CONFORMITY TO THE WORLD'S LOWER STANDARDS.

Can you imagine the reaction if someone tried to use a similar excuse about adultery?

If God truly rewards those who sincerely seek him, do you think he might actually bless the Christian leader who seeks to emulate God's generosity by stepping away from the pack to turn his or her salary package on its ear? What do you imagine might happen to productivity if your organization had the goal of providing an abundant life for everyone in its employ? How would your benefits package look if your organization were to ask, "What's the best plan we can afford to offer"?

The Bible is replete with stories of unmerited favor, of people receiving good things they didn't deserve. If God has called us to offer good to those who haven't earned it—the definition of grace—how much greater should our debt be to those who have earned more but receive less?

Jesus said, "Among you it will be different." Breaking free from the chains of conventional wisdom in this area of wages and benefits might be one of the most difficult adjustments you'll need to face, but imagine the wonderful blessing the difference will mean for your employees.

4

TIME-MANAGEMENT TRAINING CAN BE A CON GAME

> *[Jesus said,] "The harvest is great, but the workers are few. So pray to the Lord who is in charge of the harvest; ask him to send more workers into his fields."*
>
> LUKE 10:2

JESUS WAS PREPARING TO SEND SEVENTY-TWO of his followers on some short-term mission trips. Thirty-six teams would go out in groups of two to reach multitudes of people in towns and villages surrounding Palestine. It was a monumental task for such a small group of volunteers.

It's clear that Jesus understood the futility of having too few people assigned to an important job. The size of the task exceeded the limits of the available workforce, and Jesus tells his followers to pray that more helpers will join them along the way. The additional bodies were not going to come by chance; the Lord of the harvest would provide them.

We don't see Jesus urging his followers to "work smart," nor do we see him sending them to class so they can learn to use a Day-Timer. The world's most effective leader very distinctly encouraged his followers to beg for more help. I have a hard time imagining he would suggest such a thing were he not certain their prayers would be answered and that more people would be added to the effort.

Just a few pages later, Luke records a story Jesus tells about a shrewd manager who was thoroughly dishonest. He concludes the parable by telling the Pharisees, "No one can serve two masters. For you will hate one and love the other; you will be devoted to one and despise the other" (Luke 16:13).

Jesus' message is primarily about the extreme conflict we face when we try to love both God and material things, but look at it from a leadership perspective. If it's impossible to serve two masters, leaders should never put an employee in the impossible position of having to choose between one boss and another. Splitting an employee's time and attention between two supervisors will always lead to misunderstandings. It may seem like a sensible thing to do, but the untenable burden it places on the employee is both unfair and counterproductive.

Workplace studies indicate that three employees are now required to handle tasks to which five people had been assigned just a few years ago. Everywhere I turn, there are people putting in longer hours and more effort for the same or less pay because their workforce has been trimmed.

Employees who remain after a round of layoffs are encouraged to consider themselves lucky because, after all, they still have jobs. And there is some small comfort in that. But the relief turns to agony when workers realize they will have even less time with their families and will be under even greater pressure to perform.

Stress levels go through the roof as the remnant push harder to cover more work with fewer hands. Although the motive on the part of their employers is not the same, these modern-day workers remind me of the Hebrew slaves who were forced by Pharaoh to increase their output of bricks while at the same time having their supply chain for straw cut off.

RELIEF [AT NOT BEING LAID OFF] TURNS TO AGONY WHEN WORKERS REALIZE THEY WILL HAVE EVEN LESS TIME WITH THEIR FAMILIES.

There's no part of me that believes this is

what Jesus had in mind when he promised an abundant life (see John 10:10). Even those who work for ministry organizations or Christian companies can fall victim to conventional wisdom that suggests God has all this work for us to do, so we need to keep our shoulders to the wheel and "get it done," even if we become miserable and stressed out in the process. There's no way God intended for his children to be this stressed at work.

The typical response when employees express concern about the amount of extra work they face is that they need to learn better time-management skills. The rationale is that we all can be more efficient, and if

> THERE'S NO WAY GOD INTENDED FOR HIS CHILDREN TO BE OVERLY STRESSED AT WORK.

we work smarter, we can get more done in the same amount of time. The problem with this is that time management becomes a Three-card-Monte game.

Three-card Monte is a confidence game in which marks (victims) are tricked into betting they can pick the winner from among three rapidly shuffled playing cards. It is almost impossible to win because the con man is holding all the cards and moves them too quickly for the marks to follow.

Players are enticed by operators who start slowly and allow the marks a few easy wins at the beginning. Once the victims are hooked, the game speeds up to a point where the marks virtually never win. A smart dealer will slow down occasionally and give his victims hope of recovering, but that doesn't last for long. The marks are stuck on a treadmill from which there's no way to escape except to just cut their losses and jump off.

Similar to victims in a Three-card-Monte scam, employees who register concerns about having too much work and not enough time to do it are often persuaded the problem is their own lack of time-management skill rather than an institutional strategy to squeeze more work out of fewer people. The employees are stuck in a no-win situation that is totally beyond their control.

LEADERSHIP RE:VISION

Your role as a leader includes the responsibility of providing for and protecting the people God has called you to lead. If there is more work for them to do than they can adequately handle, you need to either provide more help or eliminate some tasks. Accomplishing your organization's goals at the expense of your employees' lives and health is not an example of godly leadership, no matter how admirable your goals might be.

Asking employees to make bricks when

they have no straw or to choose between one or more masters might resonate with conventional wisdom, but I can't imagine it rings true from God's perspective.

Perhaps it's time to think about praying to the Lord who is in charge of the harvest and asking him to send you more workers or give you fewer fields to manage.

5

BE ALERT FOR HUGE MISTAKES

24

*When the cool evening breezes were
blowing, the man and his wife heard the
LORD God walking about in the garden.
So they hid from the LORD God among
the trees. Then the LORD God called to the
man, "Where are you?"*

*He replied, "I heard you walking in the
garden, so I hid. I was afraid because I was
naked."*

*"Who told you that you were naked?"
the LORD God asked.*

GENESIS 3:8-11

HUMAN BEINGS ARE PRONE TO MAKING MIS-
takes. Some of us seem to specialize in certain
types of errors, but all in all, the tendency to
screw up is part of our DNA. You might even
call it a universal *core competency*.

Mistakes come in all shapes and sizes.
Most are rather inconsequential and easy to
fix (thank goodness for spell-checking software!). Some, like traffic accidents, are more
severe, but they are commonplace to the
point that we have systems in place to miti-
gate their consequences.

Then, there are the doozies, those colossal goofs that come out of nowhere to take your breath away. Blunders that leave you speechless. Legendary faux pas.

Adam made the ultimate mistake when he ate the fruit Eve had given him. The course of human history was eternally altered by Adam's lapse in judgment, and God punished him (and us) for it. But there's a key leadership lesson in the way God honored him, despite the incredible error he'd committed.

God had given Adam a direct command: Don't eat from the fruit of that tree. Adam disobeyed. It can't be any more cut and dried than that.

There are a handful of examples throughout the Bible where the text is written in a way that seems to *suggest* God isn't all-knowing and that he doesn't have all the answers. This is one of them. God walks into the Garden and calls out for Adam, as if he doesn't know where Adam is—and what he's done.

I think God did this to teach us lessons. We certainly aren't omniscient, so God is showing us—through practical example—how we are to act in similar situations.

Adam hides from God, and when he finally does reveal his whereabouts, God gives him a chance to tell his side of the story.

In the wake of an act of direct defiance, God still honors Adam by allowing him to speak first. And Adam says, "I heard you walking in the garden, so I hid. I was afraid because I was naked."

And even after Adam responds with a lie, God gives Adam another chance: "Who told you that you were naked?"

LEADERS LEAD

You know that the people you lead are going to make mistakes. You can set up systems to reduce the incidence of error. You can train. You can adopt all sorts of quality-control programs, but employees are still going to make mistakes—little ones, careless ones. Doozies.

God's approach to Adam indicates that his first priority is to honor the relationship he has with Adam. There's no evidence of a scorched-earth response. God doesn't strike Adam dead, although he certainly would have been justified in doing so. He simply states the consequence of Adam's action and moves on. I wonder if God's gracious approach gave Adam the courage to draw near to God at later times in his life.

GOD'S FIRST PRIORITY WAS TO HONOR THE RELATIONSHIP HE HAD WITH ADAM.

God didn't allow Adam's blunder to stand in the way of his mission. From the beginning of time God desired to have a relationship with his creation. Adam's sin didn't change that. The structure of the relationship was altered, but God's desire for one was not. The rest of the Bible tracks the story of God's continued interaction with humankind.

How Do You Handle Mistakes?

Do people on your team hide from you because they are afraid of your reaction? Do you ignore them as if nothing has happened? How has your reaction to errors affected the fulfillment of your company's mission?

Good leaders have contingency plans for situations outside their control. Maybe you've spent time thinking about what you would do if a major supplier were no longer available or how you'd handle the loss of a significant client.

DO PEOPLE ON YOUR TEAM HIDE FROM YOU BECAUSE THEY ARE AFRAID OF YOUR REACTION?

Considering the propensity of people for making mistakes, you need to set aside time to think about, and plan your reaction to, a major blunder by a trusted employee. Better yet, do some role-playing with your top leadership team. Surprise them at your next meeting by announcing that one of the organization's managers has made a serious mistake, and do a practice drill. When they've finished, tell them that the scenario was not real but rather a dry run on a situation that very well might happen in the future. The role-playing will give them something to refer to if (when) they need to react to an actual emergency.

LEADERSHIP RE:VISION

Conventional leadership ideals try to avoid mistakes and reduce errors, but there's a real benefit to be gained by keeping your eye out for those times when employees stumble and fall. It's in these situations where you have a tremendous opportunity to show your team that the mission is not more important than the people who are working hard to achieve it.

The most important and long-lasting lesson from the story of Adam's first sin is the value God placed on the relationship he had established with Adam.

Don't wish for mistakes, but keep your eyes open for them and the relational opportunities they represent.

6

TELL THEM WHAT
YOU LIKE

Carefully determine what pleases the Lord.   29

EPHESIANS 5:10

HAVE YOU EVER PLAYED THE GAME TWENTY
Questions? One player thinks of a person,
place, or thing, and the others try to ascer-
tain what or who it is by asking a series of
questions—no more than twenty in all. Answers can be only yes or no. Each time players get a yes answer, they get to ask another
question. It's the yes answers that drive the
game forward.

Let's imagine that you and I are playing
the game and you have chosen to think of
an elephant. I ask, "Is it an animal?" You
answer yes, and I can now focus on guessing
which kind of animal because that one yes
answer has already eliminated every other
possible category. The field is narrowed, and
I am much more likely to guess correctly in
future questions.

Suppose I had asked, "Is it a mineral?"
Your answer would be no, and I would be no

closer to determining the correct answer because there are so many other things it *could* be. All I know is one of the things it's *not*.

Yes answers allow me to add one more valuable piece to the puzzle. No answers tell me only which pieces I can't use.

What if you try playing the game but reward the no answers instead of the yeses? You can still play, and the game will eventually end, but it will take a lot longer.

From the earliest pages of his book, God reminds us that he wants his people to please him. We're only up to Genesis 4 when we read that Cain and Abel both offered sacrifices and "the LORD accepted Abel and his gift, but he did not accept Cain and his gift" (vv. 4-5).

It is possible for God to be pleased with us. And it's possible for us to know how to please him.

Paul writes to the Ephesian church and urges them to carefully determine what pleases the Lord. And it makes sense that God would inspire Paul to write such a suggestion only if it were actually possible to know what pleases God. A loving master would never praise obedience and not provide the means for knowing what could be done to fulfill the requirement.

GOD DOESN'T HIDE BEHIND A CLOAK OF MYSTERY WHAT PLEASES HIM.

God doesn't hide what pleases him behind a cloak of mystery, and as a Christian leader neither should you.

LEADERS LEAD

It must be a misguided sense of humility that causes Christian leaders to camouflage their own preferences and force the people who report to them to play Twenty Questions when they're trying to determine what pleases the boss.

By definition, leaders are those whom others follow. It is difficult to follow someone if all you know is where they don't want to go. Imagine being a taxi driver and having your passengers tell you only where they don't want to go.

"Where to, folks?"

"Well, I can tell you for certain we don't want to go to the shopping mall."

Remember Twenty Questions? It's the yes answers that move the game along. A critical element in getting people to follow you is telling them where you want them to step and what you'd like them to do. Leaders who focus on what shouldn't be done aren't

> IMAGINE BEING A TAXI DRIVER AND HAVING YOUR PASSENGERS TELL YOU ONLY WHERE THEY DON'T WANT TO GO.

leading. They're merely drawing a line in the sand and telling their people not to cross it.

LEADERSHIP RE:VISION

Do the people you have been charged with leading know what pleases you, or do they have a *better* idea of what you *don't* like? Which would be easier for your staff to list: your five most-favorite things or your five least-favorite things? Which are you quicker to point out: the things that went wrong in a project or the things that went right?

There are situations that call for you to tell your staff what not to do. But these should always be joined with a suggestion for an alternative. If you tell someone to stop doing something without offering an alternative, you create a vacuum that needs to be filled with something else. Good leaders are clear about what that something is. Ineffective leaders force their people to waste time trying to figure out what they're supposed to do. They have a clear picture of what to avoid, but they have no idea about where to go.

Nothing about being a servant-leader precludes you from voicing your preference and opinion related to the way you want things done. The term is not *servant-follower*.

As a servant, you focus on the needs of others, of those you are called to serve. As a servant-leader you focus on the needs of your team. One of your staff's primary needs is for you to lead them—to show them what to do and where to go. They do not need you to tell them *how* to do their jobs. If you have been skillful in hiring the right people, they are better at their specific tasks than you are, so don't get into the weeds and slow your people down. Leaders lead.

No one leads by standing on the sidelines and watching the parade go by. If you are called to be a leader, you serve by leading, and you lead by clearly stating where you believe the organization should be going.

To be a true servant-leader, you need to step up and tell people what they can do to please you.

7

PAY THE FULL PRICE

34   *David said to Araunah, "Let me buy this*
      threshing floor from you at its full price. . . ."
      "Take it, my lord the king, and use it as
      you wish," Araunah said to David. . . .
      "I will give it all to you."
      But King David replied to Araunah,
      "No, I insist on buying it for the full price."

      1 CHRONICLES 21:22-24

KING DAVID HAD BECOME GREEDY FOR POWER, and even though the nation of Israel was at peace, he ordered the head of his army to conduct a national census. Ordering the census was an act of sinful pride on David's part. His military commanders told him so, but David insisted, and the census was conducted.

Unlike a modern-day census where the gathered data is used in a variety of political and commercial applications, David's action caused great hardship to the people because it conscripted all the able-bodied men into the army—and caused God to burn with anger against David and the people.

The process lasted nine months. When it

was over, "David's conscience began to bother him," and he repented for "doing this foolish thing" (2 Samuel 24:10).

The Lord brought punishment in the form of a deadly plague. David begged God to end the suffering, and Samuel writes that God "relented" when the death angel was standing over a plot of land owned by Araunah the Jebusite.

Through Gad, a prophet, God told David to build an altar on the land, and Samuel records the dialog that took place between the king and the landowner.

At first glance it might appear that David is being a poor steward by insisting that he be allowed to pay full price. The seller was willing to give the land to David for nothing. Shouldn't the king have taken the offer and used the money he saved for something else? Wasn't it foolhardy to refuse such a deal? Or was God using this exchange as a way of teaching us about another form of stewardship?

Haggling over the price or accepting the offer of free land would have devalued the transaction and dishonored all involved. In response to Araunah's offer, David replied, "'No, I insist on buying it, for I will not present burnt offerings to the LORD my God that have cost me nothing.' So David paid him fifty pieces of silver for the threshing floor and the oxen."

If a buyer persistently quibbles over the price of something and eventually beats the seller down, the result is often a lopsided deal in which the buyer is the "victor" and the seller is the "loser." Outcomes like that don't glorify the God who places love for others near the top of his priority list.

GOD IS SERIOUS ABOUT HIS DESIRE TO HAVE A RELATIONSHIP WITH US, AND HE HAS PROVED IT BY THE PRICE HE WAS WILLING TO PAY.

Paying anything but full price can also send a message that the buyers are less than serious about the value of the items or services they are acquiring. At the beginning of 1 Samuel 7, Israel has been in mourning for twenty years because their sin has separated them from God's favor.

The Jewish leaders come to Samuel and ask what it will take for them to return to the Lord, and Samuel tells the people, "If you are really serious about wanting to return to the LORD, get rid of your foreign gods and your images of Ashtoreth (v. 3)." In other words, the genuineness of your desire will be marked by the price you are willing to pay. God is serious about his desire to have a relationship with us, and he has proved it by the price he was willing to pay—the life of his Son.

LEADERS LEAD

You're the leader. Your attitudes permeate the entire organization. The way you treat vendors and suppliers trickles down and has a direct effect on the way others perceive your company. Are you known for your hard-bargaining stance and your winner-take-all approach to negotiations? Do you honor sellers, or do you beat them into submission?

And what's the end result of a hard-driven deal? What do you really gain when you nail the deal but damage the

DO YOU HONOR SELLERS, OR DO YOU BEAT THEM INTO SUBMISSION?

relationship? If your every breath is meant to glorify God, what do you say about that deep breath you take as you tighten the screws on a supplier's salesperson who will be forced to give up some commission in order to close the deal with you? God gave everything he had to buy you out of bondage. Is he really pleased when you put the squeeze on someone else for another half point?

LEADERSHIP RE:VISION

We really do have our wires crossed on this one. I know quite a few wonderful folks whom I consider paragons of godliness—except for this penchant they have for haggling over prices. The stories they tell make me squirm. One guy (a pastor) kept pounding on a used-car salesperson to get a lower price until he acquiesced. Afterward, the pastor bragged, "I would have paid more, but I was on a roll."

Wow! Is that really God's idea of stewardship? How honored did the seller feel when it was over? We leave an aroma everywhere we go. What word do you suppose that guy would use to describe the aroma of dealing with Christians after his encounter with the pastor—*stench*, maybe?

This idea that good stewardship is somehow linked to driving hard bargains has become deeply woven into the fabric of our modern zeitgeist, our moral and cultural climate. And we negotiate that way without even thinking. Breaking this automatic habit will require commitment, serious effort, and frankly, prayer.

Begin by understanding that you serve a God who places a higher priority on honoring people than he does on the amount of money in your bank accounts. Remember that God did not haggle over the price he paid for you. His willingness to pay full price was proof of the high value he placed on the object of his desire—you.

If your practice is to start demanding a lower price before you even hear the seller's offer, stop and ask yourself, *Can I afford to pay the asking price?* When a seller offers a fair price, one that's within your budget, honor him or her by agreeing to it. The benefits will go well beyond your bottom line.

8

GIVE THEM BULLETS

[Jesus said,] "You will receive power when 39
the Holy Spirit comes upon you. And you
will be my witnesses, telling people about
me everywhere."

ACTS 1:8

MY WIFE, RHONDA, ACCUSES ME OF HAVING watched every single episode of *The Andy Griffith Show* at least a hundred times. She's probably correct, although I would say in my defense that I have a lousy memory and don't always remember how the stories play out. That said, I think I should be allowed to watch the *Andy Griffith Show* marathon on TV Land as often as it comes on.

The series centers around Andy Taylor, the aw-shucks, laid-back sheriff of Mayberry, a small town in North Carolina. In true 1960s-era TV style, you can always count on Sheriff Taylor to apply an ample dose of common-sense wisdom to whatever predicament befalls the town or its people. And no one is more likely to get into a jam of some sort than Taylor's hapless deputy, Barney Fife.

Now Andy's a smart guy, but I find fault with one key element of his leadership. Sheriff Taylor's deputy, Barney Fife, is allowed to carry a pistol, but Andy won't let him have any bullets—except the one he carries in the shirt pocket of his uniform. The badge, uniform, and pistol give him the outward appearance of authority, but when it comes right down to it, Barney is a toothless tiger. He has nothing to back up his appearance of authority. And that's Andy's fault. Even though Barney is the quintessential sitcom buffoon, you should never give someone a job without providing the authority and tools needed to get it done.

NEVER GIVE SOMEONE A JOB WITHOUT PROVIDING THE AUTHORITY AND TOOLS NEEDED TO GET IT DONE.

Jesus was preparing his followers for the task he'd set before them. Having instructed them to go everywhere and share the story of his love, Jesus told them they would receive power and authority for their task from the Spirit of God. He also assured them that they would not be heading out on their own. Unlike Barney Fife, they would have plenty of "bullets" in their "guns."

Paul writes, "God has given us different gifts for doing certain things well" (Romans 12:6). When Moses left his brother, Aaron, and Hur in charge while he went up the mountain, he announced the assignment to the elders of Israel, publicly handing his authority to Aaron so there'd be no misunderstanding among the people.

Whenever God has a job for you to do, he gives you everything, including the authority you'll need, to get the job done. Can you even imagine God saying to Noah, "I want you to build a huge boat and gather some animals into it, but you'll need to figure out for yourself how to do those things"?

> WHENEVER GOD HAS A JOB FOR YOU TO DO, HE GIVES YOU EVERYTHING YOU'LL NEED TO GET THE JOB DONE.

LEADERS LEAD

As your organization navigates the path that leads to the future, you have people on the team who are sent out or brought in to accomplish certain tasks. These people are charged with extending the organization's authority and ability to wherever these things are needed.

Your team will be much more effective—and you'll be far more pleased with their results—if you provide the clear power and authority they need in order to do what you've asked them to do. Sending them out with empty guns is more than a waste of time. It sets them up to fail on your behalf—which is not pleasant for your employees or for you.

When King Artaxerxes sent Ezra the priest back to Canaan to administer the affairs of Israel on the king's behalf, he sent with Ezra an official letter spelling out the fact that Ezra had the king's authority to do his job (see Ezra 7:11-26). With the letter in hand, Ezra said he felt encouraged and headed to Canaan, confident he could accomplish the assignment (see 7:28).

LEADERSHIP RE:VISION

If you're like most people in leadership positions, you have too many things on your plate. Too much to do. Not enough time to get it all done. You've undoubtedly been to time-management courses or read books that encourage you to off-load some of your responsibilities onto someone else—and you should do more of that.

Now here's a tip for actually making that work: When you delegate responsibility, make sure you also pass along the authority to do the job. Telling others they have a task to complete is not enough. If you are going to hold them accountable for completing the assignment, they must also have the requisite power and authority. Too many organizations are packed with people who are held accountable for things without being given any real authority to gather necessary resources and get the job done.

Take an active role in handing off the project. Stop and consider the roadblocks you would face if you were responsible for the project, and then give your designated surrogates whatever they need to succeed. The least you should do is make a public announcement of the transfer so everyone involved will know you have passed responsibility and authority to someone else.

Granting your authority to someone else does not diminish your own but rather, extends it into situations you can't possibly handle on your own.

9

TELL THE TRUTH
ABOUT BAD NEWS

44

> *[The prophets and priests] offer superficial treatments for my people's mortal wound. They give assurances of peace when there is no peace.*
>
> JEREMIAH 6:14

> *How can you say, "We are wise because we have the word of the LORD," when your teachers have twisted it by writing lies?*
>
> JEREMIAH 8:8

GOD TELLS JEREMIAH THAT HIS CHIEF COM-plaint against the leaders in Israel is their habit of twisting the law to fit their own agendas. He is angry at them for using truth to support untruth.

God seems to be especially angry with his prophets and priests, because they are leading people astray with half-truths and falsehoods built on truthful foundations. What they are saying is *factually* correct; it just isn't *completely* correct.

While I was writing this, a prominent U.S.

politician was defending himself against accusations that he had lied about an opponent's voting record. When reporters pressed him to explain his obviously inaccurate statements, he countered with an assertion that everything he said was *factually* correct (his emphasis).

No one I know was buying that explanation. That politician was as transparent as a cellophane bag, but

WHAT THEY ARE SAYING IS *FACTUALLY* CORRECT, IT JUST ISN'T *COMPLETELY* CORRECT.

45

he got away with making those statements because he was "correct." Everything he said about the other candidate was truthful—to a point. On further analysis, it became evident that certain key elements of the story had been left out, elements which, if included, would have led to a completely different conclusion.

Which is worse: using the truth to support a lie, or flat-out lying?

Have you ever been handed a shocking dose of reality by learning the complete truth about a situation you thought was heading in a totally different direction? The all-too-frequent stories of large companies whose management has cooked the books and left unsuspecting investors holding the bag are obvious examples of this, but there are plenty of less-newsworthy scenarios taking place every day.

No one will argue with me when I advocate for a greater level of truth telling, but the practice of such truth telling may be further from reality than you've considered. Omitting portions of the truth can be as harmful as telling a lie. Choosing to remain silent in order to avoid conflict will eventually result in unfortunate misunderstandings.

Being honest when it comes to bad news may not be the most expedient approach, but it's the right thing to do. Having to tell your staff that you may have to sell one of your warehouses is not a pleasant thing, but failing to tell the truth isn't leading, it's manipulating. Omitting portions of the truth isn't being truthful.

Telling the truth about bad news might cost you valuable employees. On the other hand, if you aren't straight with them about the bad news and you eventually have to fire them, you've gained nothing, and you've dishonored them in the bargain. In God's eyes, your relationship with your employees is far more important than the loss of a warehouse. When viewed through those criteria, telling the truth, no matter how painful, just makes sense.

Early in my career I was given the responsibility of managing a business for absentee owners who had made some monumentally foolish decisions and had brought the operation to the edge of insolvency. As cash flow began to enter a death spiral, my bosses demanded that I keep a happy face and not tell the staff what was going on. But I couldn't do that.

The news was bad, and if the owners were unsuccessful in their final desperate effort, just about everyone on the team would have to be let go. I gathered the staff together and explained what was going on: Sales are up. Expenses are down. We would be in great shape were it not for a deep hole we are trying to climb out of.

Most of my staff weren't surprised. Some openly admitted that they had been getting their résumés in order. Everyone was relieved to have someone acknowledge the elephant in the room. In the end, the owners' Hail Mary pass did work out, and they sold the business. Most of the staff members were retained by the new company, and I was let go because they couldn't afford my position. Despite the frustration of all that, knowing that I honored those folks with the truth has been one of the highlights of my professional career.

LEADERSHIP RE:VISION

Perhaps the most difficult place to tell the complete truth is during staff performance evaluations. It's so difficult that many otherwise decent leaders choose to lie to their staff and tell them everything is hunky-dory. Just fine. No need for concern.

I think this may be more of a problem in Christian organizations because the concept of grace has been skewed to the point of suggesting that we shouldn't point out faults or shortcomings in someone's performance. We have the idea that being nice is preferable to being truthful.

WE HAVE THE IDEA THAT BEING NICE IS PREFERABLE TO BEING TRUTHFUL.

If you have staff members who aren't cutting it or who need to exhibit dramatic improvement, it's your duty as a leader to tell them the truth, the *whole* truth. Speak lovingly, but tell the truth (see Ephesians 4:15). As the leader, it's your responsibility to take the organization forward. If an employee's performance isn't contributing to the effort, you are falling short of your own calling by ignoring the issue.

Leaders must do what only they can do. And only leaders can come beside staff members who aren't measuring up and help them see where they need to improve. Anything short of this is dishonoring to those employees, who deserve to know the truth for the sake of their own growth and for the good of the organization.

10

Be Ignorant; Ask Good Questions

[The Lord says,] "Forget all that [I've done before]—it is nothing compared to what I am going to do. For I am about to do something new. See, I have already begun! Do you not see it? I will make a pathway through the wilderness. I will create rivers in the dry wasteland. . . . Yes, I will make rivers in the dry wasteland so my chosen people can be refreshed."

Isaiah 43:18-20

At the time Isaiah records these words, God is on the verge of bringing Israel out of exile in Babylon. The people, including Isaiah, are most likely circulating stories about the many ways Yahweh has conquered their enemies in the past. Everyone is getting excited. They're anticipating the work of God's mighty hand once again.

Will God send a swarm of hungry locusts? Will the Babylonian rivers run red with blood? Will the angel of death pass over the land and destroy the Persians' firstborn children?

God says no. That was then, and this is now. The solutions of yesterday are not the answers for today. "I am about to do something new" (Isaiah 43:19).

Conventional wisdom suggests that a sensible course of action is to find something that works and keep doing it. Most organizations scorn the idea of reinventing the wheel as a frivolous waste of time. So why does God, who orchestrated the successful exodus from Egypt, tell the Israelites to *forget all that* and look for him to do something new?

Perhaps it's God's way of telling them they should never be satisfied with the status quo. His motive may be to attack their complacency by bringing about their deliverance in a completely different manner. No one knows the mind of God, so I won't even try to guess his reasons. It's enough to focus on the fact that the God of all creation chose to do something new (one translation calls it "a brand-new thing"). Brand-new things are about the future, about moving forward, about ignoring what worked in the past and looking for something that will work even better in the future.

IGNORE WHAT WORKED IN THE PAST AND LOOK FOR SOMETHING THAT WILL WORK BETTER IN THE FUTURE.

Many people consider Peter Drucker the father of modern business consulting. His thoughts and ideas have probably influenced more business decisions than have any one else's. There's a business school named for him. A friend of mine was a student there and actually had Drucker as an instructor. To this day, that remains a highlight of his life.

Drucker says his greatest skill as a consultant was to be ignorant and ask good questions.

He isn't talking about playing dumb or in any way minimizing his intellect. He's advocating an approach where knowledge about the past should be subjugated to intelligence gathered about the future.

Asking questions—asking *good* questions—forces you to ignore what you've learned and to seek new answers from what is going on now and from what might be going on tomorrow.

LEADERS LEAD

There's an unfortunate misconception that leaders are the ones with all the answers. Some actually buy into that misconception and are burdened by what I call the Paradox of Success, a malady that tricks leaders into thinking they can rely on good decisions made yesterday to solve problems caused by tomorrow's situations.

You are suffering from the Paradox of

Success if you repeatedly reach into your bag of yesterday's successful answers. You are a victim of success if you rely on data from surveys or experiences that have been on the shelf long enough for you to have memorized their contents. If you think you know more about your customers than a new hire who hasn't had your vast years of experience, you are a prime candidate for an "I'm a Victim of My Own Success" button.

Paul warned the church at Corinth, "Anyone who claims to know all the answers doesn't really know very much" (1 Corinthians 8:2). The Corinthians had been arguing over whether or not followers of Jesus were allowed to eat meat that had been sacrificed to idols. Some in the church were standing on long-held principles, and others were questioning traditions that prohibited the practice.

Without taking a definite side, Paul ignores the traditions of the past and presents a well-reasoned set of questions that can help individuals determine the answer that is proper for them. As a leader in the new church, Paul is providing a perfect example of *being ignorant and asking good questions*.

LEADERSHIP RE:VISION

History is valuable only when it is used as a guideline for formulating today's questions in search of answers for tomorrow's situations. The past becomes dead weight when previous solutions are applied solely on the merits of their earlier success. What worked yesterday will work tomorrow only if the situations are identical—and they almost never are.

Look for new ways to do things, even if everything is going well. When employees or board members ask why we need to change, turn the tables and ask them to show you what value there is in maintaining the status quo. Just smile and say, "Why do we need to keep doing things the same way?"

THE PAST BECOMES DEAD WEIGHT WHEN PREVIOUS SOLUTIONS ARE APPLIED SOLELY ON THE MERITS OF THEIR EARLIER SUCCESS.

Learn to ignore what you learned yesterday and ask good questions:

- What is the latest we've heard from the field?
- What are we doing that no longer makes sense?
- Are we in a rut? If so, where?

Every time we meet, my friend who studied under Peter Drucker asks the same question: "What are you reading?" His thirst for new ideas is never quenched. He tells me we're friends because I keep bringing him new ideas, and the feeling is mutual. He is always stretching me beyond my comfort zone with ideas I've never even heard of.

If you need a perfect example of someone who ignored the answers of the past and asked good questions, look at Jesus. As you spend time in the Gospels, you'll see a leader who challenged the status quo at every turn and asked some of the best questions you'll ever hear.

11

QUIT PLAYING
IT SAFE

Caleb tried to quiet the people as they   55
stood before Moses. "Let's go at once to
take the land," he said. "We can certainly
conquer it!"

NUMBERS 13:30

MOSES HAD LED THE ISRAELITES TO THE EDGE
of the land they'd been promised, and now it
was time to scout out what lay ahead. God
told Moses to pick one man from each of the
twelve ancestral tribes and send these twelve
to check things out. So Moses sent them out
with these instructions: "See what the land
is like, and find out whether the people living there are strong or weak, few or many"
(Numbers 13:18).

The scouts did as they were told. At one
location, "They cut down a branch with a
single cluster of grapes so large that it took
two of them to carry it on a pole between
them!" (Numbers 13:23). The place was incredible—all God had promised and more.

When the men returned to Moses after

forty days, they told him of a magnificent country "flowing with milk and honey" and offered the gigantic grapes as proof of the region's bounty (Numbers 13:28). But ten of the men warned that trying to move forward would be too big a risk. The inhabitants of the land were huge: "We can't go up against them! . . . Next to them we felt like grasshoppers" (13:31, 33). They had counted the cost and found they didn't have enough faith to achieve the goal they'd been working toward since leaving Egypt.

At this point, I imagine that Moses turns to Caleb, who'd probably been standing a few feet apart from the other men. "Son of Jephunneh, what do you have to say?"

I can see Caleb standing there, feeling very much alone. Every eye on him. He clears his throat and then boldly replies, "Yes, the people are giants, and they won't give up easily. But I think we should try, anyway. Did you see the size of those grapes!?"

LEADERS LEAD

Leading is about taking people and organizations to places they are not currently, and it's also about breaking the stranglehold of the status quo, under which so many groups suffer. Human beings are incredibly adaptable, and they often choose to stay where they are, as uncomfortable as it may be, to avoid the risk of going to a new place or taking on a new idea.

On the verge of winning the prize they had been seeking, the Israelites were seriously talking about choosing a new leader and going back to Egypt. Even after they had been given a first-hand account of the benefits that lay ahead, they were not willing to take the risk. They wanted to play it safe.

LEADING IS ABOUT BREAKING THE STRANGLEHOLD OF THE STATUS QUO.

Good leaders refuse to be crippled by the threat of risk. Having a healthy respect for the challenge is certainly necessary—Caleb didn't ignore the size of the people—but he looked beyond that to the treasure that lay ahead. Playing it safe isn't leading; it's following the will of the group's lowest common denominator. It's turning your eyes away from the original vision and accepting something less than the full reward of success.

But leaders are nothing without willing followers, so sharing your vision of a "land flowing with milk and honey" is critical. The people must *want* to go where you've asked them to go. Effective leaders take great pains to sell the benefits of their mission. Perhaps one of the most famous examples of this occurred in 1961, when President John

F. Kennedy shared his vision of "landing a man on the moon and returning him safely to Earth" by the end of the decade.

Kennedy told Congress that "no single space project in this period will be more impressive to mankind . . . and none will be so difficult or expensive to accomplish." He recognized the risk but, like Caleb, placed greater value on succeeding than on playing it safe.

LEADERSHIP RE:VISION

God wants you to step out and take risks, depending on him to provide the safety net of faith you need. Knowing that God is watching your back gives you the confidence to make bold decisions. Isaiah told the Israelites, "The LORD will go ahead of you; yes, the God of Israel will protect you from behind," as they were preparing to make the journey from Babylon back to Zion (Isaiah 52:12).

Christian leaders too often hide behind the guise of good stewardship and do whatever they can to avoid any chance of failure. Church boards are afraid to set budgets that exceed last year's giving because doing so isn't prudent. Instead of asking, "What awesome things do we think God has in mind for our ministry?" they reject big ideas because "there's no way we could afford to do that."

Jesus didn't play it safe, and neither should you. Luke records Jesus talking about the risk involved in being his disciples, telling them not to follow him "until you count the cost" (Luke 14:28).

Too many Christian leaders use this verse to argue for "realistic goals" and plans that are more about maintaining the status quo than about moving forward into the future God has prepared for them. But Jesus isn't saying that difficult missions should be avoided. On the contrary, he *wants* people to carry their own crosses as they follow him. If you need an example of a leader who didn't shy away from difficult choices and unpopular paths, you needn't look any further than Jesus.

JESUS DIDN'T PLAY IT SAFE, AND NEITHER SHOULD YOU.

But what if the future is so unclear that you can't even see the finish line? What if you've taken a step of faith but the results just aren't forthcoming? Do you back off and retreat to the predictable plans of the past, or do you recognize the risk and press ahead?

Isaiah faced a similar dilemma. He knew that God had chosen him for a specific task and had called him "from within the womb," but the prophet was frustrated: "My work seems so useless! I have spent my strength for nothing and to no purpose" (Isaiah 49:1, 4).

But through his disappointment at things that weren't moving as fast as he would have liked, Isaiah remained faithful to the God who protected him: "Yet I leave it all in the LORD's hand; I will trust God for my reward" (49:4).

If you've been playing it safe, stop following the past, and look to the future God has waiting for you. Don't stifle the awesome plans he has for the people he's called you to lead.

12

It's All about the Future

Samuel then took a large stone and placed it
between the towns of Mizpah and Jeshanah.
He named it Ebenezer (which means "the
stone of help"), for he said, "Up to this
point the LORD has helped us!"

1 SAMUEL 7:12

I focus on this one thing: Forgetting the past
and looking forward to what lies ahead.

PHILIPPIANS 3:13

THERE'S A LOT OF HISTORY IN THE BIBLE.
God starts his book with a history of the
creation of the universe. He goes all the way
back to *the beginning*. You can't get any
more historic than the moment it all started.
There's no prehistory in the Bible because all
history started when God created time—in
the beginning.

All along the way, God directed his people
to stop and mark specific occasions so they
could remember where they had been and
what they'd been through. The Sinai Desert

was dotted with Ebenezers raised in acknowledgment of significant milestones.

After the Israelites crossed the Jordan, God instructed Joshua to choose twelve men, one from each tribe, and send them back into the river. Each man was to pick up a stone and carry it out on his shoulder. These stones were then fashioned into a memorial so future generations would be reminded that "the Jordan River stopped flowing when the Ark of the LORD's Covenant went across" (Joshua 4:7).

Genealogies, step-by-step construction notes on the Temple, detailed descriptions of previous events—the descendants of Israel were obsessed with their own past. In Jesus' day, Hebrew children could recite long passages of history from the Torah. Indeed, the Temple rabbis were blown away by young Yeshua's (Jesus') detailed knowledge of history.

And yet all that history became worthless because it blinded the people to what—who—was coming and eventually did come. They were so firmly focused on their history that they ignored the future they had longed for when it arrived. History can be extremely valuable if you use it to help you reflect on the future. Knowledge of what

ALL THAT HISTORY BECAME WORTHLESS BECAUSE IT BLINDED THE PEOPLE TO WHAT—WHO—WAS COMING.

happened yesterday is nothing but dust in the wind if it isn't used to influence what could happen tomorrow.

God is all about the future.

Don't Look Back

Who isn't intrigued by the story of Lot's wife? When God destroyed the towns of Sodom and Gomorrah, he wiped them out completely, leaving nothing. Only Lot and his family were allowed to escape.

An angel gave Lot's family specific instructions to not look back as they fled the conflagration. The angel didn't give a reason, but the message was unmistakable: *Don't look back*. Nevertheless, Lot's wife, for some inexplicable reason, looked back and became a pillar of salt (see Genesis 19:26).

Now, I wonder why God included this story in his book. There are plenty of other instances where people were punished for disobeying instructions much more serious than "Don't look back." Did God give us this little narrative to teach us a lesson about paying too much attention to where we've been and not enough to where we're going? Could it be that the story of Lot's wife is there to show us that God doesn't want us to dwell on or live in the past? that he wants us to set our hearts on him and keep moving forward?

LEADERS LEAD

One role of leaders is to encourage others to go places, do things, or consider ideas that are different from the places, things, or ideas that make up their status quo. Leaders move us forward by providing a vision of what is to come. Leaders can be students of history, and doing so is valuable if it keeps them from repeating the mistakes of the past. But if they are to lead effectively, their focus must be on the future.

Effective leaders, real leaders, are often more comfortable dealing with the future than they are with the present. Genuine leaders are wired to what could or should happen tomorrow. They are rarely comfortable with things as they are.

Paul the apostle had a colorful past. He had a tremendous pedigree and a thorough knowledge of Jewish history. He had also been connected with some of the darkest moments in the young church's recent past: Paul had been present at the stoning of Stephen and before his own conversion had zealously persecuted the believers. But after encountering Christ on the road to Damascus, he chose to forget (to not dwell on) those

> GENUINE LEADERS ARE WIRED TO WHAT COULD OR SHOULD HAPPEN TOMORROW.

things and to focus his energies on looking forward to what lay ahead.

As a leader, you must focus on the future, on what is beyond the horizon. Put managers in place to take care of today. Charge them with maximizing the status quo while you explore what you can find around the corner.

LEADERSHIP RE:VISION

It's important to mark milestones, as Joshua did after crossing the Jordan River. It's even more important to leave the milestones behind, for those who come later, and move forward.

Every step you take is preparation for the step you are *about* to take. If God is a God of hope (and I believe he is), then God is the God of tomorrow—because hope is all about what will happen next.

When the children of Israel were safely on the far side of the Red Sea, they celebrated. The women danced and played tambourines while everyone sang songs of praise and thanks to God. They had made it safely out of Egypt. Mission accomplished.

But in the very next verse we read that Moses led the people of Israel away from the Red Sea and into the Shur Desert. The initial mission had been accomplished—time to move on.

Effective leaders are always looking for the next assignment. Leaders who focus their attention on the past and try to build their plans on what worked yesterday are like drivers who try to steer their cars by looking only in the rearview mirror.

Too many Christian leaders have become enamored with the past. Instead of marking a milestone and moving on, they fight tooth and nail to protect the status quo, to stay where they are. Churches that changed and tried new things as they grew in the 1980s and 1990s are now wondering why their models are no longer working. Businesses that posted great gains in years past and are no longer doing so are blaming everything and everyone but their own inability to adjust to new ideas and strategies. Afraid of upsetting a cart that carries fewer and fewer apples, they resist the idea of change and hold steadfastly to yesterday's solutions, at the expense of tomorrow's result.

The Latin phrase *Carpe diem,* translated "Seize the day," encourages us to not let a single day go to waste. It's about grabbing what we can of today.

I like the Spanish/Latin twist on that phrase—*Carpe mañana*—translated as "Seize tomorrow." To me, it communicates a proactive attitude. Don't just allow the future to come crashing through the window; rather, understand that everything you do today will have an effect on how tomorrow turns out.

You can't do anything about yesterday, but you can—and should—build a foundation for tomorrow. God chooses not to "remember" our past or hold it against us and has wonderful plans for our future. Leaders should follow his lead and do the same.

Good Leaders
Are Self-ish

What do you benefit if you gain the whole world but are yourself lost or destroyed?

Luke 9:25

I sometimes imagine that heaven has a gallery displaying billions and billions of paintings, each one portraying the specific life God planned for each of his children as he knit them together in their mothers' wombs. I can see him walking through this incredible exhibit, stopping along the way to look and smile (or wipe away a tear) as he reflects on how his creations have lived the lives he fashioned for them.

Now, I know that's not theologically accurate, but I also know beyond any doubt that God has a specific plan for my life, a plan that requires individual aptitudes and traits that he planted in me before I was born. There's too much evidence to think otherwise.

God told his people through Jeremiah, "I know the plans I have for you" (Jeremiah 29:11).

Jesus reassured his disciples of the Father's care, telling them that "the very hairs on your head are all numbered" (Matthew 10:30).

And Paul went to great lengths in more than one letter to help us understand God's attention to detail in our formation by giving each of us specific gifts and abilities.

DAVID WAS AWARE OF THE *SELF* GOD HAD GIVEN HIM.

69

There's more, and all of it points to a Creator who took the time to craft each human being with an unduplicated individuality. It isn't just our fingerprints and DNA that are ours and ours alone—it's our very souls.

King David is described as being a man after God's own heart. It's clear that David was aware of the *self* God had given him. Even as a young boy, David knew who he was and who he wasn't. When Saul's soldiers gave David a suit of armor to fight Goliath, he refused and took only his sling, because that's who he was.

When Jesus called Peter and Andrew to leave their father's fishing boat, he didn't ask them to become anything other than what they were already. They were fishermen. Jesus merely asked them to fish for a different kind of catch.

Each of us is unique. In God's amazing creativity, he handcrafted our personalities and talents into packages

EACH OF US IS UNIQUE—GOD HANDCRAFTED OUR PERSONALITIES.

that are specifically suited for the tasks he has in mind for us.

LEADERS LEAD

Michael W. Smith's song "Place in This World" speaks to a universal lament:

> *Looking for a reason*
> *Roaming through the night to find*
> *My place in this world*
> *My place in this world*
> *Not a lot to lean on*
> *I need your light to help me find*
> *My place in this world*
> *My place in this world.*

That "my place" is different for each of us, and Smitty's song resonates with so many people because we ache to live the life God mapped out for us.

I am happiest when I am smack-dab in the middle of God's plan for me. In the summer of 2001, I was reading John Eldredge's *Wild at Heart* when I realized that the prestigious and well-paying job I had was the result of my putting my *self* on a shelf and gaining the world by trying to be someone I wasn't. We were doing great Kingdom work, and I was a valued member of the team, but the guy whose name was on my paycheck was not the guy who looked back at me from the mirror every morning. I was grouchy and spinning in a state of perpetual burnout.

Christ's admonition about those who gain the world but lose their souls had a spiritual meaning for me, but something in *Wild at Heart* clicked with me, and I knew I had to make some changes in my life. I knew I was not honoring the *self* God had in mind when he painted the picture of my life for his gallery.

Perhaps the most famous example of someone living the life God designed is Eric Liddell. In the film *Chariots of Fire*, Liddell's family has always presumed that he would follow in the footsteps of his missionary parents in China. But he starts to run track in college and, for a time, forsakes family tradition in order to participate in the Olympic Games. When pressured by his sister for an explanation, Liddell shows that he has clearly found his place in this world: "I believe God made me for a purpose, but he also made me fast. When I run, I feel his pleasure."

There is nothing more tragic than people who have lived their lives trying to please everyone else when they should have been trying to celebrate the *selves* God had in mind for them.

Consider Jonah, who did everything he could to avoid living the life God had planned out for him. Can you think of anything more miserable than being swallowed alive by a huge fish—and living to write about it?

Jesus, on the other hand, knew exactly what his Father wanted him to do. Indeed, Jesus told his followers, "My nourishment comes from doing the will of God, who sent me, and from finishing his work" (John 4:34).

LEADERSHIP RE:VISION

This leadership thing isn't easy. There's a delicate balance between being the *self* God intended and becoming self-absorbed. The more time you spend in conversation with God, the better able you'll be to see his purpose for your life.

Rick Warren started *The Purpose Driven Life* by stating, "It's not about you," yet with respect for the great work Pastor Warren has done, it really is *all* about you.

God created *you* to handle a specific assignment on his behalf. If he's put you in a leadership position, take the time to examine your *self*. Do you have a good understanding of the abilities and aptitudes God gave you? Are you using them to the fullest? Are there things you are marginally good at that could be much more effective if you took the time to practice them? Do you have personality traits you've kept hidden in an effort to gain the world? Are you following a plan designed by someone who doesn't know or care about you as much as God does?

If God took the time to knit you together, with all the personal attention that image represents, isn't it sin to ignore his design and act out a completely different part?

Take the time to find out who you really are. Elephants don't climb trees. Nor do giraffes. But both animals eat leaves. Each goes about the task of eating leaves in the specific way God intended.

Your leadership efforts will be more effective if you lead with an understanding of the *self* God gave you.

14

Manage Your Image

[Jesus said,] "If I were to testify on my own behalf, my testimony would not be valid. But someone else is also testifying about me, and I assure you that everything he says about me is true."

John 5:31-32

Jesus Christ, whom John described as full of grace and truth, is telling a group of religious leaders that his own words of affirmation won't be enough to convince them of his deity. *He* knows who he is. He knows that he is speaking the truth, but Jesus turns to a third party to validate his claims.

The exchange comes as religious leaders are criticizing Jesus for breaking Sabbath rules. They have also heard him refer to God as his Father, which in their understanding places him as God's equal (see John 5:16-18). The charges are serious, and Jesus knows he can't just say, "Look, my word is my word, and that's all I'm going to say."

Instead, Jesus directs their attention to John the Baptist, who was respected as a person of integrity. He says, essentially, "You trust John; let him vouch for me."

Jesus knew the value of a good reputation or public image, and he took steps to manage the timing of certain elements surrounding his growing celebrity. He was aware that premature exposure would confuse some people and could stand in the way of the relationship he was developing with his closest followers.

After healing a leper, Jesus urged the man to first visit the local priest and offer the traditional sacrifice, but the man ran through town shouting about Jesus at the top of his lungs. The result, writes Mark, was a throng of people so large that Jesus could no longer enter the town publicly (see Mark 1:40-45).

After giving two blind men their sight, Jesus warns them—*sternly,* says Matthew—"Don't tell anyone about this" (Matthew 9:30).

Christ's purpose in coming to earth went beyond making lame men walk and blind men see, and the image management we read about in the Gospels points to the true heart of Jesus. He wanted people to know him as more than an itinerant prophet who healed the sick.

LEADERS LEAD

It doesn't show up on your P&L (profit and loss) statement. You won't find it listed among your tangible assets, and you don't consider it part of your company's intellectual property, but your image is the most valuable thing you own. It's also one of the most difficult assets to control.

You have insurance to protect you against loss. You set aside reserves to cover costs when business goes soft. You might cross-train your staff in anticipation of personnel changes. But there isn't a policy anywhere that will restore a sullied reputation or fix a poorly managed image.

Good corporate reputations don't just happen. You have to *work* at building them.

Perhaps the best rule of thumb comes from the book of Proverbs, which says, "Where there is no vision, the people perish" (Proverbs 29:18, KJV). With just a bit of stretching, we could adapt the statement to mean that when people don't have enough information, they make stuff up to fill in the information gap. And when people "make stuff up," they tend to assume the worst.

WHEN PEOPLE MAKE STUFF UP, THEY TEND TO ASSUME THE WORST.

As humans, our minds have a natural tendency to dwell on worst-case scenarios whenever we lack sufficient information. So if you don't want your corporation's image to fall apart, be proactive. Give those around you adequate information. Don't unwittingly provide opportunities for their minds to wander where you'd rather they not go.

Don't Hide Your Light under a Bushel

The best approach is to maintain a consistent stream of positive releases about your organization's activities. A steady diet of good news can help to build a defensive shield against negative attacks. Everything you say or do as an organization adds to the mosaic of your image. If there is such a thing as an insurance policy against an image crisis, it probably has something to do with previous proactive efforts to tell your story.

Don't hide your light under a bushel. Take a lesson from Jesus as he spoke with the religious leaders, and find a credible third party to help you tell your story.

LEADERSHIP RE:VISION

The most common excuse for not maintaining an effective image-management program is a faulty sense of what true humility is. In a misguided effort to appear humble, Christian leaders will shun the glare of publicity and say something like, "We'll let our reputation speak for itself."

The problem with this is that it doesn't follow the examples God included in the

Bible. Jesus encouraged his followers to let their light shine among men so that all might see their good works and glorify God. The apostle Paul frequently sought situations where he could speak or debate theology before throngs of people.

Remaining quiet while the public waits or

clamors for an explanation can easily be interpreted as a sign of having something to hide. If you have legitimate reasons for saying nothing, step up to the podium and say that. There are times when saying that you are unable to elaborate on a particular point is part of an effective image-management plan, but being completely silent is seldom a good idea.

SAYING SOMETHING LIKE, "WE'LL LET OUR REPUTATION SPEAK FOR ITSELF" DOESN'T FOLLOW THE EXAMPLES GOD INCLUDED IN THE BIBLE.

Your responsibilities as a leader include stewardship of the organization's most valuable asset—its image. And a good image is worth everything you own. Everything is replaceable except your image. God has given you a burning-bush imperative to lead. Don't squander his blessing by taking a lackadaisical approach. If you conduct regular meetings to review the company's financial status, then also invest an appropriate amount of time examining and planning for the maintenance of your most valuable asset.

People are going to talk about your organization. That's a given. Do what you can to ensure that what they are saying is the truth.

15

STAND IN THE SPOTLIGHT

80

The LORD told Joshua, "Today I will begin to make you a great leader in the eyes of all the Israelites. They will know that I am with you, just as I was with Moses."

JOSHUA 3:7

TAKE A MOMENT TO PICTURE THE ENTIRE nation of Israel camped on the banks of the Jordan River. Not one of the people assembled has any firsthand knowledge of life as a slave in Egypt. Every person who was part of the Exodus has died, including Moses, who had led the people for forty years.

Tomorrow morning, a special group of Levitical priests will take up the Ark of the Covenant and start to walk across the Jordan and into the Promised Land. In the morning, the Israelites will go to a place they have never been. They are going someplace new, and God has selected Joshua to lead them.

Joshua hasn't sought this role. He hasn't been campaigning for it. Joshua is a soldier, and like most military men, he is happy to simply do his job and follow whatever orders he's given.

But God has a different plan for Joshua. Yahweh is going to set Joshua apart. He is going to elevate this soldier to a position of recognition and fame. The spotlight of leadership is about to shine squarely on Joshua, not because God wants to honor Joshua, but simply and practically because the people can't follow someone they cannot see.

Scripture is sprinkled generously with stories of leaders who stood in the spotlight of their time and did what was required. Moses stood above a battlefield with his arms outstretched. As long as he was there with his arms out, the Israelite army enjoyed victory (see Exodus 17:8-13).

Joseph and Daniel both accepted prominent leadership positions in the courts of kings who served pagan gods. Although David and Solomon had different leadership styles, they were held in high esteem by their people. Even while Saul was still king, the people sang songs praising David's victories.

IF PEOPLE CAN'T SEE YOU, THEY CAN'T FOLLOW YOU.

The lesson woven through all these examples is the need for leaders to be visible. If people can't see you, they can't follow you.

At one point in my life I was blessed with the opportunity to lead music for a growing church with a wonderful tradition of great worship. I started as an occasional singer in a small team of people who stood up front and sang. We weren't really leading, just "following from the front." Over time, and because of some health issues among the others, my participation grew more frequent until I was up front every week and many in the congregation began to think of me as the worship leader.

Not wanting to grab the spotlight from others who had also been part of the group from the start, I suggested to the pastor that we rotate leaders. We talked about it for a few minutes, and when he sensed that I was genuinely trying to act out of humility, he gave me some advice that has shaped my leadership perspective ever since.

"Jim," he said, "you *are* the leader; you just need to accept that and lead." He explained that my suggestion of rotating music leaders would be similar to his wanting to rotate senior pastors. When I suggested that I didn't want folks to think I was hogging the spotlight, he half-joked that I could try leading from the front pew—as long as people could follow me from there.

I think this is where I picked up the idea of leading from a burning-bush imperative. Moses stood before the burning bush, and God gave him the authority to go and liberate the Israelites. Moses hadn't sought the "celebrity," and he even tried to tell God that he might not be the best choice. Nonetheless, God used the bush to get Moses' attention and to drive home the point that he was God's choice to lead the people out of Egypt.

It's not easy to keep things in balance. Isaiah writes that "human pride will be brought down, and human arrogance will be humbled" (Isaiah 2:11), so it helps to have people around you whom you trust to warn you when you've gone too far. The key to keeping your humility in perspective while standing up front is to see what you're doing—or what God is doing through you—as a way to bless others (see Genesis 12:2).

LEADERSHIP RE:VISION

It doesn't come up in everyday conversations, but people really do need leaders. When things go wrong, we usually don't shout, "If only we had someone to lead!" We're more apt to scramble for solutions to problems than we are to search for effective leadership, but we're certainly eager to follow just about anyone who says he or she has a plan for the future.

Luke describes a leaderless scene in Ephesus: "The people were all shouting, some one thing and some another. Everything was in confusion. In fact, most of them didn't even know why they were there" (Acts 19:32).

Without leaders, people are doomed to wander aimlessly, often not even knowing why they are where they are.

Perhaps you have been sitting behind the curtain, just offstage, watching and waiting for someone to stand up and take charge. What if the someone they're all waiting for is you?

WITHOUT LEADERS, PEOPLE WANDER AIMLESSLY, NOT EVEN KNOWING WHY THEY ARE WHERE THEY ARE.

Take heart from the story of Deborah, a prophet who became a judge in Israel. She was not power hungry and did not seek a leadership role, but when she saw that she was needed, she stepped up and led Israel in a decisive battle.

When the fighting was over, Deborah and a military leader named Barak sang a song that should give you some encouragement: "Israel's leaders took charge, and the people gladly followed. Praise the LORD!" (Judges 5:2).

Your spotlight is waiting—step into it.

16

MUST WE ALL GET ALONG?

In his grace, God has given us different gifts for doing certain things well.

ROMANS 12:6

Some of us are Jews, some are Gentiles, some are slaves, and some are free.

1 CORINTHIANS 12:13

How strange a body would be if it had only one part!

1 CORINTHIANS 12:19

ALLOW ME TO IMAGINE WHAT HEAVEN MUST have been like when God was bringing the earth into existence. Out of a timeless infinity, the Creator of Everything stepped into time and started painting from a limitless palette. We know from Genesis that God merely spoke and things happened.

I wonder what it was like to have been an angel watching all this happen, especially on the days when God created birds, fish, and animals. Imagine the whirlwind of color and excitement:

Look, there's one with red wings and a blue tail, and one with green feathers and a yellow head.

Oh my. That one in the water has purple stripes, eyes that bug out, and a tail that flips up and down rather than back and forth.

Can you believe all the different things he created to eat? Some are sweet, and some are sour. Have you heard about the banana? It's yellow, and you can't eat the skin the way you can an apple.

My point is that God "went wild" and created a world full of diversity. The variety is almost endless. Even today, scientists are finding new plants, animals, and other living things they didn't even know about before.

It's no different with God's most-favored creation. Scripture says each of us was knit together in our mother's womb. The God whose imaginative powers fills museums with countless species of butterflies made every human being unique.

As I wrote in chapter 13, it's not just our fingerprints and DNA that set us apart; it's our personalities—our souls. There is not another person on the planet who is exactly like you.

When I was doing the research for this chapter, I was struck by the amount of attention Paul focuses on this idea of diversity, of being different. One of the apostle's recurring themes is that God made each of us different and that we are subsequently made one through the Spirit of God.

Paul never argues for us to ignore our uniqueness but to use the strength of our diversity for the benefit of all.

LEADERS LEAD

Near the end of John's Gospel he records a long prayer in which Christ entreats God the Father to bring unity among his followers (see John 17). He doesn't ask God to make them all the same but rather asks that they would have the same objectives despite their diversity.

It's impossible to know the mind of Jesus, but I sometimes wonder whether he might have been thinking of Matthew and Simon, two of his handpicked disciples. Matthew had been a tax collector for the Roman government—the very symbol of Roman oppression over the Jews in Palestine. Simon was a member of the Zealots, a radical political group dedicated to the violent overthrow of Rome.

If Jesus was so committed to unity among his followers, why did he handpick two men of such opposing perspectives as part of his inner circle? Why invite the disagreements that certainly must have occurred between

Simon and Matthew? I'll bet there were some doozies.

Jesus knew that populating a team with differing opinions and experiences is the best way to take advantage of the power of God's creative genius. We aren't all created different because God became bored with one model and decided to try something else. We are diverse because God, in his infinite wisdom, knows that our differences will add to the mosaic in tangible ways that no other combination of personalities can.

> TAKE ADVANTAGE OF THE POWER OF GOD'S CREATIVE GENIUS.

LEADERSHIP RE:VISION

If your team sings "Kumbaya" at every meeting, you have a problem. If two or more people always agree on everything, at least one of them is redundant.

Peter and Paul disagreed fiercely over issues facing the early church, and yet God blessed them both. Lack of diversity results in *incestuous amplification*, a situation in which people with shared opinions and perspectives feed off one another and become convinced that their ideas are the correct ones. Without the benefit of a contrary view, members of the group amplify their positions to unreasonable, and often tragic, conclusions.

Why do we always assume that disagreements will end in division? Demanding that everyone share similar views is an affront to the creativity of the One who made us different in the first place.

What criteria do you have for selecting members of your team? Look around the table. On a scale with diversity at one end and sameness on

DEMANDING THAT EVERYONE SHARE SIMILAR VIEWS IS AN AFFRONT TO THE ONE WHO MADE US DIFFERENT IN THE FIRST PLACE.

the other, how does your team stack up? Do you have a Matthew *and* a Simon?

In Acts 13:13, we read that John Mark left the company of Paul and Barnabas and returned to Jerusalem. There's speculation as to why, but what you don't see is God's displeasure at what may have been a difference of opinion. Both Paul and John Mark were blessed with full ministries, and their writings are part of the Scripture we read today. If they didn't march along to the beat of the same drum, there's no reason to require the members of your team to do so.

When was the last time someone on your team was passionately opposed to one of your ideas?

When you put an important team together, look for people who don't come from the same place as you. Hire from outside your industry. Instead of asking, "So, are we all in agreement on this?" look around the room and challenge someone to disagree: "Come on, there must be at least one of you who has a different idea."

If the ideas coming from your leadership team are feeling a bit cold, remember that friction creates heat.

17

WHEN WINNING ISN'T

Pay careful attention to your own work, for then you will get the satisfaction of a job well done, and you won't need to compare yourself to anyone else. For we are each responsible for our own conduct.

GALATIANS 6:4-5

THE MOST COUNTERINTUITIVE ELEMENT OF my Leadership RE:Vision concept is the idea that leaders should not set the goal of being *number one* but rather the goal of being *excellent*. God is much more interested in personal-best trophies than he is in first-place ribbons.

People who set their sights on being first, biggest, strongest, or any number of similar superlatives will struggle with the words of Jesus when he suggests that the first will be last. Those whose primary objective is to be the best—even when they have the most noble of intentions—will have difficulty with the scriptural mandate to celebrate the success of others. How can you want to be the best and still pray that the other guy wins?

Paul writes that "we are each responsible

for our own conduct" (Galatians 6:5). If we can't control our competitors' performance, why set as an objective anything even related to a comparison of our outcome with theirs? Instead, follow Paul's advice, and strive for personal excellence in everything.

When Jesus tells the parable of the demanding master who gave his servants various amounts of money to invest, he praises the one who had the greatest return, but he also recognizes the second servant because he had done his work to the best of his abilities. If winning were everything, the second servant would not have heard his master say, "Well done!"

LEADERS LEAD

The key to success is having control of your own goals and objectives. Playing a game where someone else is allowed to move the goalposts is a losing proposition.

Olympic pole-vaulters set their sights on a little bar about eighteen feet in the air. They run at a precise speed, hold their poles in just the right way, and place one end in the exact spot needed to propel themselves up and over the bar. Imagine how fruitless their efforts would be if someone were allowed to move the bar up or down a few inches in the middle of the jump.

Setting goals you can control is a much better way to measure success. Doing so puts you in control of your own conduct and allows you to focus on your own team's performance rather than on that of your competitors.

The CEO of XYZ Widgets wanted nothing more than to outsell his competitor, Wimple Widgets. The XYZ leader pushed his team to the limit. "Our goal is to overtake Wimple Widgets and become the world's number one supplier of hand-polished, double-twisted widgets," he reminded them over and over again.

What a year they had! The best in company history. The celebration was on—until *Widget Weekly*, their industry trade paper, published year-end statistics indicating that Wimple had outsold XYZ by three-tenths of a point and was still the industry leader.

Despite their stellar performance, the XYZ team felt defeated because they had been shooting for a goal they could not control. If XYZ's leadership had set goals that were within their power to control, such as increased performance and internal excellence, the celebration would have continued, and the team would have enjoyed "the satisfaction of a job well done," as Paul wrote in Galatians 6:4.

One of the best examples of someone who paid attention to his own conduct is Nehemiah, with his dedication to rebuilding the wall around Jerusalem. Nehemiah didn't blindly ignore the bad publicity his project was receiving, but neither did he let it change his plans. He focused on getting the wall built, and he allowed nothing to get in the way of his goal.

When you watch and react to your competitors' every move, you are allowing them to set your agenda. But when you set *personal excellence* goals, you can win regardless of other companies' performance.

There's certainly nothing wrong with desiring success. In fact, God wants to bless you with success. But he wants your priorities to be aligned with his.

LEADERSHIP RE:VISION

Inherent in having the goal of being the best or number one or the market leader is the fact that doing so requires everyone else to "lose." There's only one first place, and if "being first" is your goal, you're asking for everyone else to lose. You win. They don't.

On the other hand, *excellence* is a position that can be shared by many. If you strive for excellence or a personal best, you can reach your goal regardless of the per-

THERE'S ONLY ONE FIRST PLACE. IF "BEING FIRST" IS YOUR GOAL, EVERYONE ELSE LOSES WHEN YOU WIN.

formance of your other competitors. If "excellence" is your goal, everyone wins when you reach your goal, they can reach theirs, too. Everyone wins.

It's not semantics.

95

> IF "EXCELLENCE" IS YOUR GOAL, EVERYONE WINS WHEN YOU WIN.

First place is all about me. The benefit is internally focused. Being the market leader in your industry doesn't necessarily translate into a benefit for your customer. The building blocks for success could actually include things that are detrimental to the customer. The fact that you sold more widgets than anyone else could mean that you lowered the quality and dropped the price.

In contrast, excellence is all about the customer. The benefit is externally directed. If your organization's goals are to provide excellent quality, unequalled customer service, and unmatched value, the customer wins when you reach your objectives.

The key to making all this work in a God honoring way has a lot to do with motive.

Your definition of success may need to be altered. Is winning the race your goal, or is achieving a personal best the real measure of success? As a leader, you should desire success not for what it can do for you but for how you can use it to bless others.

18

PUSH AWAY
FROM THE TABLE

[Jacob told Esau,] "Please take this gift I have brought you, for God has been very gracious to me. I have more than enough." And because Jacob insisted, Esau finally accepted the gift.

GENESIS 33:11

IT'S BEEN YEARS SINCE JACOB TRICKED HIS father, Isaac, into giving him the birthright of his older brother, Esau. Jacob has been living with his father-in-law and is now returning to his homeland. He doesn't know quite how Esau will react, so he sends gifts ahead, and when they finally meet, he has even more presents for his older brother.

The gifts Jacob has for Esau are meant as a peace offering, but I am struck more by what Jacob says than by what he does. Jacob uses a phrase we don't hear much these days: *I have more than enough*.

He accurately credits his good fortune to God's generosity, because he knows he would have nothing were it not for God's provision. Everything he owns has come from God.

This ability to say enough is enough must be a family trait. Jacob's grandfather Abraham did the same thing to his nephew Lot when the two of them were trying to divide some land. Abraham and Lot went to the top of a mountain and surveyed all the land God had made available to them. As the elder of the two, Abraham could have pulled rank and demanded first choice, but he told Lot that he could take his choice of any section of the land he wanted and then they would separate (see Genesis 13:8-9).

Abraham had enough, and he resisted the temptation to amass an even greater fortune by insisting on getting his fair share.

Paul cautions against the sin of greed, which he equates with idolatry (see Colossians 3:5). Jesus encourages us to consider the lilies, who do no work and yet are clothed with the beauty they've been given (see Matthew 6:28-29). On the other hand, entire

PAUL EQUATES GREED WITH IDOLATRY.

books have been written and countless sermons preached about biblical characters who allowed greed to get the better of them.

No one will ever argue in favor of greed, yet among too many leaders it has become a common trait.

Organizations need to grow and move and change to remain healthy. If your organization isn't expanding to attract new customers or to serve new people, you will eventually suffer the pangs of entropy as you slowly—or not so slowly—shrink into nonexistence. Growth and profits are elements critical to success.

However, an obsessive desire for expansion can result in corporate obesity and a full complement of problems ranging from budgets that are stretched so thin there's no room for even the slightest error to employees who are overburdened to the point where they can't help but make mistakes.

It's easy to fall into the "more is better" trap. Following the pack is easier than making up your own mind. When a competitor rolls out a new product, the simplest response is to follow along and bring out one of your own. Remaining competitive and relevant to the market is a good thing, but when a company moves ahead with a "me, too" product without first determining the level of customer need or corporate ability to deliver, you have the first steps of greed gone wild.

Rapid expansion isn't always a bad thing, and there are some incredibly large organizations that handle their monstrous size quite well, but they are the exceptions rather than the norm. More common are huge companies that look great on the outside while hiding massive problems just beneath the surface. This occurs so frequently that any names I'd list here would be old news within a matter of months.

Effective leadership is about taking people to places they've not been, guiding an organization to new levels of achievement, earning greater profits, *and* doing so in a way that leaves the organization healthier than it was when the journey started. Running the people and the business into the ground for the sake of growth is not a definition of success.

LEADERSHIP RE:VISION

I am amazed by the exemplary self-control many leaders display in their personal diet and exercise regimens. Some of these folk are downright obsessive about their physical well-being. I usually see them coming in from their early morning runs while I'm standing in line for a ham-and-cheese croissant at the hotel breakfast counter. I save room in my bags for my special pillow. These dedicated souls pack running shoes.

If you are one of these, I salute you. Help yourself to another bowl of bran flakes while I google the nearest place to grab a chili dog.

Sad to say, though, many of these same

physically disciplined people have yet to conquer their corporate appetites and need some personal training on how to say, "No thanks. We have enough."

Using stockholder and investor pressures as an excuse is no more valid than my blaming a lousy diet on the difficulty of eating properly on the road. There are alternatives to a Big Mac Extra Value Meal, and there are opportunities to step off the insatiable corporate treadmill. The grilled chicken sandwich may be less satisfying to my taste buds, but I'll be healthier in the long run. Curbing your appetite for unhealthy growth will require adjustments, but just like choosing the grilled chicken, you know it's the right thing to do.

WE NEED PERSONAL TRAINING ON HOW TO SAY, "NO THANKS. WE HAVE ENOUGH."

Revising your leadership approach is about looking at things through different lenses and from fresh perspectives. In that light, consider this: Knowing when to say you have enough is also about being generous. When you push away from the table, you give others an opportunity to get a share of the pie. Using your size to gobble up everything in sight limits what others can do.

You might be at a tough spot on this one, stuck between the rock of needing to make a living and the hard place of wanting to control your appetite. Take comfort in the assurance that you are not alone. Sociologists are beginning to see evidence of a strong trend toward personal and even corporate restraint.

Try starting a conversation with a few close friends by saying, "You know, I am beginning to think I have more than I need." Their responses might surprise and encourage you.

19

EAT WITH
THE TROOPS

Don't be selfish; don't try to impress others.
Be humble, thinking of others as better than
yourselves. Don't look out only for your own
interests, but take an interest in others, too.

PHILIPPIANS 2:3-4

THERE IS SOMETHING ABOUT SHARING A
meal that brings people closer together. The
special bond we experience when eating together probably has its roots in a time when
food was less easily obtained than it is today.
The need for food was a great equalizer, and
total strangers were welcomed as part of the
family out of necessity.

The backdrop of Scripture is dotted with
times of meal sharing, such as the visit to
Abram by three men, one of whom is tra-
ditionally believed to have been the Lord
himself. When the three visitors come to
see Abram, he tells his wife, Sarai, to make
bread from the best flour. He kills a fat calf
and spreads a feast for his guests.

Elijah visits a widow who has only a small

portion of oil and flour, but because she uses the last of it to make bread for the prophet, her supply never runs out, and she always has enough to eat.

The Gospels record two incidents where Jesus feeds huge crowds of people from a small amount of available food. One of the pivotal episodes in the life of Christ is commonly called the Last Supper, and one of his postresurrection appearances is to his disciples on the shore of the Sea of Galilee, where he is cooking fish for them to eat.

Luke writes that one of the early church's first decisions was related to how food distribution would be carried out. These are just a few of many examples where food plays a supporting role in the biblical narrative.

In all of these stories, and in others, there is another common thread: The act of sharing a meal brought together people of differing social status. Heavenly visitors eat with Abram. A widow shares bread with a prophet. Jesus feeds the masses.

Today, the act of sharing a meal is less about the need for food and more about the need for a break

MEALTIME CAN BE A GREAT EQUALIZER, ESPECIALLY IN THE WORKPLACE.

from whatever it is we're doing. But it can still be a great equalizer, especially in the workplace.

LEADERS LEAD

If you had the time to chat with managers and employees at large and small organizations all over the world, you'd find that one of the most common concerns they have is lack of communication. Does that sound familiar?

Here's a simple way to improve communication: Bosses and workers should eat together more often. I'm not talking about formal lunches or dinners with predetermined agendas and someone taking notes, but rather the simple act of opening a sack, taking out a sandwich, and enjoying the camaraderie of sharing a meal with other humans. Good communication is built on good relationships, and lunch is a good time to relate.

Lunch is a time when coworkers catch up on details of their personal lives that might not be appropriate for discussion in the office. Parents share stories of their kids' illnesses and school concerns. Sports fans review questionable calls from a televised game. Someone asks the IT girl about a problem on a home computer. The talk is casual and generally non-work related. If there is talk about work, it's usually more informational and is almost always tucked in right at the end, as people are gathering up their paper sacks.

I give you this travel guide to the employee lunchroom because it may have been some time since you paid a visit and you need to understand the culture. You may own the lunchroom and sign the paychecks of everyone at the tables, but the lunchroom is their turf, and you are the alien.

LEADERSHIP RE:VISION

A devotion that encourages managers to bring a sack lunch and eat with their staff in the lunchroom might typically focus on the first half of the Scripture reference at the beginning of this chapter, but this is a book about thinking differently, so I want to point out the benefit of the second half. (Go back and read the verse.)

Eating with the troops can be a tremendous thing if you use the time to relax and enjoy the company of other people. As Paul instructed the Philippian church, this is a time to set aside your own agenda and show interest in theirs and what they are doing.

How long has it been since you sat with the staff and had lunch? If it's been a while, the first couple of times might be tricky. Remember, you are invading their turf. If they sense you are arriving with an agenda, they'll be polite, but you won't enjoy the benefit of strengthening relationships.

Don't ask a lot of questions. And don't be surprised if you're treated with a bit of deference the first few times. I suggest you make this a regular occurrence. If you do, the atmosphere will warm up, and soon they'll be saving you a seat at their table.

Back to the verse: The purpose for your lunchroom visit is to strengthen relationships with your team. You are there to learn what is important in their lives, especially the lives they lead away from work. You're there to soak up the culture of the people who have traded their talents and their time to help you achieve your objectives.

YOU'RE IN THE LUNCHROOM TO SOAK UP THE CULTURE OF THE PEOPLE WHO TRADE THEIR TALENTS AND TIME TO HELP YOU REACH YOUR GOALS.

The key to success is the first half of the verse. Approach the table with humility and grace. Think of the painting *Christ at Heart's Door* and the gentleness with which he quietly stands, waiting to be invited in.

If anyone has a right to force an entrance, it's Jesus, yet he stands waiting to be asked in: "Look! I stand at the door and knock. If you hear my voice and open the door, I will come in, and we will share a meal together as friends" (Revelation 3:20).

This is one of those simple things that can

make a huge difference in your organization. Approach it casually. Don't make a big deal out of it. Just show up with your brown bag and relax. You'll be glad you did.

20

HARNESS THE
POWER OF DREAMS

Jacob found a stone to rest his head against and lay down to sleep. As he slept, he dreamed of a stairway that reached from the earth up to heaven. And he saw the angels of God going up and down the stairway. At the top of the stairway stood the LORD, and he said, "I am the LORD."

GENESIS 28:11-13

GOD IS ON THE VERGE OF TAKING HIS covenant with Abraham to an exciting new level, and Jacob is going to be Yahweh's point person on this important leg of the journey. Knowing that he needs to capture Jacob's undivided attention, God provides Abraham's grandson one of the most fantastic views of heaven anyone on earth has ever seen.

God promises in the dream to protect Jacob and remain with him constantly until the covenant is fulfilled, and I can imagine this dream motivated Jacob to stay faithful through some incredibly difficult events in his life. When Jacob woke from the dream, he turned what to others might have seemed a fantasy into reality by dedicating the spot where he had slept as the gateway to heaven.

The Role of Dreams

Dreams play an important role in Scripture.

Jacob's son Joseph tells his brothers of a dream he had in which they bow down to him, and they become so angry that they sell him into slavery in Egypt. That sets the stage for Joseph to end up in a position to save his brothers from starvation during a seven-year famine.

> DREAMS PLAY AN IMPORTANT ROLE IN SCRIPTURE.

Joseph's ability to interpret dreams places him in a powerful position with Pharaoh and allows Joseph to be God's agent of salvation for his entire family.

Daniel finds favor with two Babylonian rulers because of the ability God has given him to tell the meaning of dreams.

An angel appears to Joseph in a dream to assure him that Mary is bearing a special child.

Peter has a fantastic dream in which a blanket loaded with forbidden foods descends from heaven in front of him and a voice instructs Peter to eat things that have been considered unclean since the days of

Moses. God uses the dream to change Peter's perspective on sharing his knowledge of Jesus with Gentiles.

Of course, the most famous "dreams" in history are those God revealed to John, as recorded in Revelation.

LEADERS LEAD

Dreams, whether they come from God during sleep or come as goals or visions when we're awake, carry an amazing power to motivate. Effective leaders through the ages have used dreams to spur people on to new levels of commitment and to instill excitement for difficult and uncertain tasks.

As I was writing these words, the world was commemorating the death and celebrating the life of Dr. Martin Luther King Jr. On the night before he was assassinated in Memphis, Tennessee, Dr. King delivered a speech during which he shared his dream for the future:

> We've got some difficult days ahead. But it really doesn't matter with me now, because I've been to the mountaintop. And I don't mind. Like anybody, I would like to live a long life. Longevity has its place. But I'm not concerned about that now. I just want to do God's

will. And he's allowed me to go up to the mountain. And I've looked over. And I've seen the promised land. I may not get there with you. But I want you to know tonight, that we, as a people, will get to the promised land. And so I'm happy, tonight. I'm not worried about anything. I'm not fearing any man! Mine eyes have seen the glory of the coming of the Lord!

I mentioned in chapter 18 that the very essence of leadership is taking people to new places, often to places they have never been, perhaps to places they have never even imagined. These new places can be physical realities, such as the Promised Land dreamed of by the Israelites. More commonly, leaders guide people to a new idea or a new way of thinking, such as the promised land of racial equality described by Dr. King.

The power of dreams lies in their ability to motivate. Sharing your vision of a desirable new future helps others see what could be and spurs them on. When you paint pictures of the future, as Dr. King did, you allow others to see what you've seen, making it easier for them to follow you over the mountaintop.

SHARING YOUR VISION CAN HELP OTHERS SEE WHAT COULD BE AND SPURS THEM ON.

I am going to presume that you have never aspired to be known as a dreamer. That title is generally reserved for those whose heads are in the clouds and who often have a loose grasp on reality.

Our culture frowns on business communication that is anything short of empirical. We devalue ideas that aren't backed by piles of research and data: "Show me the money!" "Where's the beef?!" "Just the facts, ma'am!"

I've seen quite a few corporate organization charts over the years, and I can't recall any of them having a box titled "Vice President of Dreams." And that's too bad.

Chances are, you have some dreamers on staff, but they're afraid to speak up for fear of joining Joseph in a cistern somewhere out in the desert, banished from any substantive dialogue because what they have to say just doesn't fit the standards of conventional wisdom.

Find these people and rescue them. They aren't hard to spot. You'll often hear them say, "I just had a crazy idea" or "Can I suggest something really different?"

Your success as a leader is related to your ability to motivate people in new directions. They are much more likely to follow if they can catch the vision for where you're headed and for what lies in front of you. Dreams can be a powerful tool in reaching your own promised land.

21

ALLOW PEOPLE TO FAIL

We can rejoice, too, when we run into problems and trials, for we know that they help us develop endurance. And endurance develops strength of character.

ROMANS 5:3-4

ONE OF THE MANY THINGS I APPRECIATE about the Bible is the way it treats the idea of failure. So many characters in biblical history have skeletons in their closets, and the amazing thing about the Bible is that it leaves the closet doors wide open for all to see what's inside.

Failure, and God's grace when dealing with it, is a common theme throughout Scripture. And the important lesson seems to be that failure is not the end of the road. The consequences of failure cannot always be mitigated, but rarely does failure stop people dead in their tracks. There's almost always a tomorrow.

The passage above, from Romans, is part of Paul's treatise on the nature of humanity and our transformation through Christ. Although failing at work may not be as serious as the trials Paul and other early Christians faced, I think we can learn leadership lessons from God's approach to failure of any kind.

One lesson is the need to get up, dust ourselves off, and get going again.

Josh 7

Joshua's army was soundly defeated by the army of Ai because Achan, one of Joshua's soldiers, had disobeyed God after a previous battle and had taken some plunder, something God had expressly forbidden. Once the sin had been revealed and dealt with, the Israelite army went back to Ai and reversed the earlier outcome in a second battle.

Another lesson is the need for leaders to see that the failure, whether sinful or otherwise, is the anomaly and to focus on an individual's ultimate potential. David sinned by sleeping with Bathsheba and then having her husband killed. God wasn't pleased, but he saw past the failure and focused on the fact that David was still a man after God's own heart.

2 Sam 11

At a critical moment, Peter denied even knowing Jesus, but Christ knew that this was a temporary lapse and eventually established his church on the man he nicknamed The Rock.

Mark 14:66-72

In each incident, and in many others

throughout Scripture, the recipients of God's mercy appear to come back even stronger than they were before, proving Paul's point that problems and trials are good for us because God uses them to produce growth.

LEADERS LEAD

Leadership is not a science. Sometimes things just don't turn out the way we planned. One of the keys to effective leadership is to keep looking forward. Learn from failures, but don't dwell on them. Examine the factors that led to the disappointment, make necessary adjustments, and move ahead.

Resist the automatic temptation to assign blame, and instead ask questions to help you determine what went wrong.

Were your plans based on faulty assumptions? Did you have bad information going in? Was the failure a result of hurried-up plans? Did your objective for the project mesh well with your mission? Was the effort underfunded? Did you have the right people in charge? How did external forces affect the outcome? Did something happen that was beyond your control?

God knew that Adam and Eve had sinned, but even then he asked questions of Adam.

Your focus should always be on the future. Use what you learn from the past to help you shape tomorrow. Ask questions about yesterday, and then use that information to help you develop solutions that will work in tomorrow's environment.

God forgives sin and erases it from his memory. In a similar manner, leaders should deal with the consequence of failures and then move forward.

LEADERSHIP RE:VISION

Do past failures haunt you or your organization? Are decisions about tomorrow held hostage by unpleasant memories of past mistakes? Perhaps it is time to move your history as far as the east is from the west. Leading is about taking the organization toward the future. You can't serve two masters. Either you are focused on the future, or you're focused on the past. The choice is yours. If you choose history, you'll need to find someone else to lead.

As you revise your leadership perspective on this, it might be helpful to explore biblical stories about

> YOU CAN'T SERVE TWO MASTERS. EITHER YOU'RE FOCUSED ON THE FUTURE, OR YOU'RE FOCUSED ON THE PAST.

people whose success came on the heels of incredible failures, people such as Peter, David, Joshua, and Moses. Paul complained about his constant struggle over doing what he knew he shouldn't and not doing what he knew he should.

God loves you. He has plans to do you good. That means he is looking out for your future. It doesn't matter what type of job you have. If you do what you do to God's glory, he wants to bless you. If you are hamstrung by an unfortunate past, ask him to help you turn your eyes toward his vision for your future.

Protect Your Young Leaders

Before I close this chapter, allow me to share a few thoughts on the need to give young leaders special attention.

Young leaders are especially vulnerable to the damage that can come from making mistakes or experiencing failure. There are times when we thrust them prematurely into projects for which they are not ready, projects that exceed their ability or their level of experience. The resulting early disasters can plant seeds of doubt that sprout dangerous weeds and become difficult to eradicate.

Jesus tells the parable of the shrewd manager and teaches that "if you are faithful in little things, you will be faithful in large ones" (Luke 16:10). Reading between the lines, you can see the importance of allowing young leaders to gain experience in small things and not placing them in situations that could destroy their spirits.

Each young leader is going to have different abilities, but it's up to you to make sure he or she doesn't burn out. Protect your young leaders. Help them balance. They are going to make mistakes. Don't set them up for failure by turning up the heat too fast.

22

RECHARGE YOUR BATTERIES

The apostles returned to Jesus from their ministry tour and told him all they had done and taught. Then Jesus said, "Let's go off by ourselves to a quiet place and rest awhile." He said this because there were so many people coming and going that Jesus and his apostles didn't even have time to eat. So they left by boat for a quiet place, where they could be alone.

MARK 6:30-32

UNLESS YOU ARE VASTLY DIFFERENT FROM most leaders, I think it's safe to assume you don't get enough rest. All but a handful of us ignore the biblical examples and fail to actually build Sabbath time into our lives. And I think the lack of R & R saddens the One who gives us everything we have.

Rest isn't optional with God. He commands it for two reasons.

First, he wants us to build time into our schedules when we put everything else aside to focus on him. In our hectic Whac-A-Mole lives, it is quite easy to forget about God and spin off into relying on our own understanding. By giving us the example of setting aside a day to rest, God is helping us to acknowledge him and keep things in perspective.

Second, he created us and knows that our bodies can't run on empty for very long before they begin to break down. God is a kind and loving Father who wants us to be healthy. Rest is essential to adequate cell regeneration, and recreation is vital for good mental acuity. He wants us to be all he imagined when he created us, and we just don't function anywhere near our full potential when we are tired or burned out.

God sets the prime example for us by resting after finishing his work of creation. It has always struck me as rather odd that an all-powerful God should need to rest, but much of what he included in Scripture is there to show us how to act. This is a clear lesson on the importance of getting off the gridiron.

In the verses from Mark 6 quoted at the beginning of this chapter, the disciples have just returned from their first mission trip. Jesus is no doubt excited to see them and to hear what they've accomplished, but he's also mindful of their need to recharge, so he leads them to a quiet place.

"The LORD is my shepherd; I have all that I need. He lets me rest in green meadows; he leads me beside peaceful streams. He renews my strength" (Psalm 23:1-3). This is the type of leader I want to be.

Leading is about taking people to new places physically, mentally, emotionally. Your responsibility is to make sure they arrive in one piece. Your efforts will amount to nothing if you reach the destination only to find the path behind you littered with the remains of those who at one time were willing to let you take them someplace they'd never been.

Perhaps it's not as dramatic as all that, but from a purely practical perspective, people make fewer mistakes when they're not tired. They perform at a higher level when they've had enough rest.

I worked for a small company that required all new employees to take one week's vacation near the end of their first six months to help them recuperate from the stress of assimilating into a new work environment. And let me assure you, on my return from that required week off, my renewed vigor—emotional and physical—more than made up for the expense associated with giving me that week off.

A friend of mine in the high-tech industry

tells stories of impromptu rubber-band fights organized by supervisors in the middle of a tension-filled push to release new software on time. Ten minutes of shenanigans can be all it takes to refresh the mind for one final push to the finish line.

One of my clients in the Midwest has a Quiet Room, where employees can enjoy subdued lighting, sit in an amazingly comfy chair, and simply chill for a while behind a soundproof door.

It's not *how* you recharge that matters; it's *that* you recharge.

LEADERSHIP RE:VISION

Where did you come up with the idea that you don't need to rest?

Do you actually believe that your work is so vital that God will look the other way while you run your body and your mind into the ground?

> IT'S NOT *HOW* YOU RECHARGE THAT MATTERS. IT'S *THAT* YOU RECHARGE.

Maybe you are trying your hardest to be a good steward of the limited time God has given you to accomplish his assignment. If so, that's commendable. But ask yourself this question: *Does God really want me to be this tired and burned out?*

Another excuse for not taking time to

IF YOU RUN OUT
OF TIME BEFORE
YOU RUN OUT OF
LIST, YOUR LIST
IS PROBABLY
TOO LONG.

recharge is a to-do list that looks as if it's been injected with steroids. Are you pridefully holding on to all this activity because you think you're *the only one who can do it*? If you consistently run out of time before you run out of list, your list is probably too long.

Learn to Say No

Do you need to learn how to say no?

The apostle Paul talks about finishing the race. Inherent in crossing the finish line is having the strength and will to keep going until you get there. If your strength and will are in short supply, turn to the One who knows you far better than you know yourself. If you're weary, ask him to lead you beside quiet waters.

God has a plan for you. He told his people through the prophet Jeremiah that his plans were "for good and not for disaster, to give you a future and a hope" (Jeremiah 29:11).

You don't need to keep going like this. Force yourself to step back, take a breath, and ask God to take control of your calendar. Ask him to help you set some priorities. Let him show you where to let go.

Follow his lead, and get some rest.

23

DEVELOP A GOOD NUMBER TWO

> *The bride will go where the bridegroom is.*
> *A bridegroom's friend rejoices with him. I*
> *am the bridegroom's friend, and I am filled*
> *with joy at his success.*

JOHN 3:29

LOOK BEHIND ANY OF THE GREAT LEADERS profiled in Scripture, and you'll see at least one strong number two standing in the shadows or lending a supportive hand to the one in the spotlight.

When God chose Moses to lead the children of Israel out of Egypt, he also brought Aaron alongside to help Moses with things he couldn't do. Aaron was apparently a much better public speaker. When Moses returned to Egypt with his assignment from God, it was Aaron who went before the Hebrew elders to tell them everything the Lord had told Moses. It was after Aaron spoke that Moses performed the miraculous signs God had placed in his hands (see Exodus 4:29-30).

Moses was a truly incredible leader. The

Pentateuch is packed with examples of his abilities, and all along the way we see Aaron's support. Moses had God on his side, but I think it's fair to say his effectiveness was enhanced by Aaron's assistance.

John's disciples were complaining that the Nazarene carpenter, whom John had recently baptized, was stealing the thunder from their guy: "John's disciples came to him and said, 'Rabbi, the man you met on the other side of the Jordan River, the one you identified as the Messiah, is also baptizing people. And everybody is going to him instead of coming to us'" (John 3:26).

John's response should be required reading for anyone in a number-two position: "I am not the Messiah. I am only here to prepare the way for him" (John 3:28). And Jesus showed, by the way he honored John's ministry, that he placed great value on John's role.

The critical need for a good number two is evident in the story of Noah. The all-powerful God of the universe decides to destroy the earth with a flood, and he chooses Noah to be instrumental in carrying out his plan. God could have accomplished the end result without anyone's help. But he found someone he could trust for the special mission and empowered him to carry out the task of building an ark.

Being a good number two is not an easy job. I've seen quite a few well-intentioned people fail at it for a variety of reasons, pride being perhaps the most frequent.

Pride

Pride comes from both directions. Failure often results when the number two wants more authority or a greater share of the limelight. But a good number two can also be inhibited by a leader who refuses to allow the helper to do what he or she is prepared and able to do. Go back to John the Baptist's comments to his own disciples, as recorded by John the apostle: "God in heaven appoints each person's work" (John 3:27). The part you play either fits into God's plan or it doesn't. I'd rather be a good number two in God's plan than a number one in my own.

Poor Communication

Poor communication is probably the second most unfortunate cause of failure for number twos, and again, it goes both ways. Leaders who clearly explain what they want and need stand a far better chance of having a number two who gets it than those who assume everyone can read their minds. We talked about this in more detail in chapter 6.

And a good number two will always let the leader know what's going on. Regular progress reports are essential. Every leader has different standards, but none of them want to be surprised by unexpected news, good or bad. Determine how your leaders want to get information, and keep a fresh supply headed their way.

LEADERS WHO CLEARLY EXPLAIN WHAT THEY WANT AND NEED STAND A FAR BETTER CHANCE OF HAVING A NUMBER TWO WHO GETS IT THAN THOSE WHO ASSUME EVERYONE CAN READ THEIR MINDS.

One of my favorite examples of the relationship between a great number two and a leader is the role Martin Sheen plays opposite Michael Douglas in the 1995 feature film *The American President*. Douglas's character is president of the United States, and Sheen is his chief of staff. The two men have known each other since college, but Sheen never calls his friend by his first name. During a heated argument about a campaign decision, Douglas yells at Sheen: "It occurs to me that in twenty-five years I've never seen *your* name on a ballot. Now why is that? Why are you always one step behind *me*?"

Sheen replies, "Because if I wasn't, you'd still be the most popular history teacher at the University of Wisconsin!"

The point is, both a number two and the

leader being served should recognize the incredible potential of such a relationship.

LEADERSHIP RE:VISION

Who is your number two? If I were to ask others in your organization the same question, would they come up with the same name?

If the name of your number two isn't obvious to you and others on your team, you don't really have one.

I'm not talking about a talented assistant who answers the phone, keeps your calendar, and knows how to reach you in the event of an emergency. There's great value in having someone like that, but a good secretary is not the same as a number two.

Number twos travel with you. They know what you know and hear what you hear. When people look at them, they see you. You trust them to make the same decision you'd make, maybe using a different skill set but resulting in the same conclusion. Good number twos stand at your side, ready to use their own unique strengths to complement your talents. They aren't clones. There's no redundancy. They don't just make you look good; they are there to make sure you are able to achieve the mission.

Think of Paul and Barnabas or Elijah and

Elisha. Both pairs had a clear leader/follower arrangement (although Barnabas initially led Paul), but it's difficult to know where the lines were drawn between them. They were as close to being of one mind as two people could be.

EVEN THE MASKED MAN HAD A STRONG NUMBER TWO AT HIS SIDE.

Too many leaders try to emulate the Lone Ranger, forgetting that even the masked man had a strong number two at his side. Scripture is sprinkled with examples of leaders who had good number twos, because God wants you to see how valuable such a relationship can be.

Has God placed someone within your circle that might fill this critical role for you?

24

Play Chess, Not Checkers

[Naomi] cared for him as if he were her own. The neighbor women said, "Now at last Naomi has a son again!" And they named him Obed. He became the father of Jesse and the grandfather of David.

Ruth 4:16-17

God is the ultimate long-range strategist, and most of Scripture's great leaders understood the value of allowing time to pass while their plans came to fruition. There are also examples of those who rushed ahead and looked for expedient solutions, and nearly all of those stories end in trouble or tragedy.

Queen Esther faced the annihilation of her entire race, but instead of rushing to the king with a story of deceit at the hands of Haman, she carefully set in motion a series of events that led to the king's discovering for himself that Haman was not trustworthy.

> GOD IS THE ULTIMATE LONG-RANGE STRATEGIST.

Paul encouraged the Corinthian church

to plant generously if they wanted to have a larger spiritual harvest. Farming is a common biblical theme because it fits so well with God's long-range perspective. It takes time for things—whether plants, relationships, or organizations—to grow.

Ruth was married to one of Naomi's sons. When he died, Naomi told Ruth that she was free to go and live with her own family. But Ruth refused and chose to stay with her mother-in-law. Through this set of circumstances, which had played out over many years, Ruth met Boaz, a family member of Naomi who was looking for a wife. Ruth married Boaz, and they had a son who became the grandfather of David. Jesus was born from the line of David.

Everywhere you look in Scripture, you see evidence of God's long-range planning. These stories help us understand God's unchanging faithfulness, but they also paint clear images of a mind-set that considers the long-term consequences of everything. The leadership lesson God wants you to learn from the stories of Esther and Ruth is that in the big scheme of life, *everything matters*.

LEADERS LEAD

Consider the differences between checkers and chess.

In checkers, you are required to jump your

opponent's game piece, even if doing so jeopardizes your position. In chess, captures are optional. A single chess move can result in the capture of only one opposing piece. Checkers allows for multiple captures in a single move. Playing pieces can move in many directions on a chessboard, but the direction of moves is limited during a game of checkers. Checkers is played on only one of the board's two colors; chess uses all sixty-four squares.

Winning at checkers requires speed and agility. Steadiness and contemplation are the hallmarks of successful chess play. Take a few minutes to think about these questions:

- Is your leadership style more like checkers or chess?
- Do you think through decisions with an eye toward the effect they'll have on tomorrow, or are you quick to offer solutions and move on to the next item?
- Do you rely on a standard approach to problem solving, or do you look for ideas that come from different directions?
- How far in advance do you plan?
- Do you visualize how your current activities will influence the unseen events and situations over the horizon?

All analogies unravel as you explore them, but I hope you get the picture I'm trying to paint. When it comes to leading people, you can come at it with a measured mind-set, or you can jump about the board attempting to capture as many of your opponent's pieces as you can in a single move.

LEADERSHIP RE:VISION

When I review examples of successful leaders in the Bible, they look a lot more like chess masters than checkers players.

If your problem solving resembles a checkers player running the board, stop and consider God's promise that he "causes everything to work together for the good of those who love God and are called according to his purpose for them" (Romans 8:28).

In God's perspective, everything is connected to everything else. There is a time and place for everything. Rushing to a conclusion doesn't seem to be God's style. Quick fixes and short-term solutions run counter to the examples we find in Scripture, even when motives seem to be correct.

RUSHING TO A CONCLUSION DOESN'T SEEM TO BE GOD'S STYLE.

Leaders get into trouble when they opt for what is expedient over what is strategic. King Saul learned a tragic lesson about the difference between chess and checkers when he offered a burnt offering to the Lord without waiting for a priest. He'd waited seven days for Samuel and became impatient. So he slaughtered an animal and offered the sacrifice himself—jump, jump, jump!

When Samuel arrived, he couldn't believe Saul's stupidity: "'How foolish!' Samuel exclaimed. 'You have not kept the command the LORD your God gave you. Had you kept it, the LORD would have established your kingdom over Israel forever. But now your kingdom must end'" (1 Samuel 13:13-14).

Many leaders struggle with this. They've been conditioned over time to make quick decisions. Managers are often evaluated on their ability to solve problems on the fly. But even in urgent scenarios requiring immediate action—such as an emergency—the leaders who will most successfully navigate through the storm are those who consider not only the short-term need but also the long-term consequences of their decisions.

Master chess players preparing for a match visualize every move, taking into consideration every play their opponents might make. As the match unfolds, they adjust their plans to meet their challengers' styles of play. Excellent players are seldom surprised.

And here's the best news: You don't even need to know all the answers. Leading up to the well-known "everything works together for the good of those who love God" passage, Paul assures us that "the Father who knows all hearts knows what the Spirit is saying, for the Spirit pleads for us believers in harmony with God's own will" (Romans 8:27).

There's no reason to carry the burden of decision making all by yourself. So relax, take your time, and enjoy the game.

25

FOLLOW YOUR LEADER

You will keep in perfect peace all who trust in you, all whose thoughts are fixed on you!

ISAIAH 26:3

CALIFORNIA POLYTECHNIC STATE UNIVERSITY is not far from my home in California. Most people refer to it as Cal Poly, and many locals just say Poly. The idea behind a polytechnic education is that students *learn by doing.* The emphasis on internships is higher at Poly than at most other schools of its kind.

We learn best when we can observe someone else doing what we're trying to master and then participate in the activity ourselves. The astronomical sales of some golf videos prove the value of polytechnic training (or that those who play golf are hopeless optimists who will try anything to improve their game).

Some of the greatest leadership lessons in Scripture are the stage directions woven between and through the recorded events. You can learn a lot about leadership by fixing your mind on *how* God leads. The words of God are the primary story, but the narrative surrounding those words speaks volumes about how we are to act and react.

Paul encourages us to "imitate God . . . in everything you do, because you are his dear children" (Ephesians 5:1). Little children learn to walk because there's amazing power in examples. They see their parents walking and want to be near them.

YOU CAN LEARN A LOT ABOUT LEADERSHIP BY FIXING YOUR MIND ON *HOW* GOD LEADS.

Have you watched toddlers take those first wobbly steps? Have you noticed how their little faces light up like one-hundred-watt bulbs when they see their moms or dads standing a few feet away, arms outstretched and full of encouragement? That's the role God wants to play in your leadership experience. No matter how seasoned you are as a leader, you will always find perfect peace in looking up to see God just ahead.

LEADERS *FOLLOW*

My premise in this book on finding a new perspective for your leadership activity is that God, the creator and sustainer of everything, has placed you in a special position, one that requires you to leave the relative comfort of the status quo while you look for and guide people toward new horizons.

Being out front, whether figuratively or literally, can be lonely. There are times when it feels as if you are driving ninety miles an hour at night but your headlights are bright enough for going only about fifty-five.

Leadership—good leadership—requires a significant amount of faith and confidence. It takes the strength and hope that come only from a living, breathing relationship with the One who gave you the burning-bush imperative to lead.

During interviews on the topic of leadership I am often asked, "Jim, what is the single most-important thing a leader can or should do?"

My answer is always one word: *Pray.* Then I go on to explain that it's not just a mandatory answer because I write from a Christian viewpoint. Rather it's an acknowledgment that every leader follows someone else. No one except God is out front all alone.

You can lead without God's help, and you can do so effectively—to a point. But you'll not be taking advantage of the greatest resource available to you. Why leave behind the single most-valuable tool in the box? God has laid out the path you're walking on. It only makes sense to ask him for guidance at every point.

Leaders often suffer under burdens of

doubt, fatigue, worry, indecision, loneliness, guilt, anger, and a host of other debilitating realities that hamper their ability to lead. If you're nodding your head in agreement because you experience any of these, take heart. Paul wrote, "Don't worry about anything; instead, pray about everything. Tell God what you need, and thank him for all he has done. Then you will experience God's peace, which exceeds anything we can understand" (Philippians 4:6-7).

LEADERSHIP RE:VISION

Not everyone can or should lead. Some should never lead. Some lead when they should step aside and follow another. Roles change. Situations call for new leaders. Leaders lose their authority to lead for all sorts of reasons.

Paul followed Barnabas for a while. Jesus asked John to baptize him. Saul was still king of Israel when God raised David to a prominent position. Joseph was appointed to a leadership role while he was in prison after being falsely accused of assaulting Potiphar's wife.

Perhaps you are in a leadership role and things just aren't working out. You are miserable. Your organization is floundering. People are looking to you for vision and direction, and you're as empty as a broken bowl. You're looking to God—*your* leader—for help, and nothing is happening.

Every company has its own set of unique circumstances, and every leader has his or her own particular issues, but one reason for the nothing-is-working dilemma could be that you are in the wrong role. Perhaps the best leadership decision you can make is to relinquish your position and turn the wheel over to someone else. If you truly believe in your organization's mission and you haven't been able to lead people over the Jordan River, God may be telling you it's time to consider the possibility of finding someone who can.

There are few things as painful as being ineffective in a leadership role. You are disappointing yourself and everyone else in the organization. You may even be wasting their time, the time God gave them to accomplish his work.

SOMETIMES THE BEST LEADERSHIP DECISION YOU CAN MAKE IS TO RELINQUISH YOUR POSITION AND HAND THE WHEEL OVER TO SOMEONE ELSE.

Solomon writes that "it is good for people to eat, drink, and enjoy their work" (Ecclesiastes 5:18). If you're in an ineffective-leadership quandary, chances are you aren't eating well, and you're certainly not enjoying your work.

This isn't easy, and I'm not suggesting that every rough patch in leaders' lives should be viewed as a sign that they are ill-suited for their roles. These are teachable moments between you and God.

But if you think it might be time to step aside, talk to your close associates, and talk to God about it. He wants you to find satisfaction in the life he's given you. He'll give you the courage to do what you need to do.

26

MAKE PEOPLE
LAUGH AND SING

*There is nothing better for people than
to be happy in their work. That is why we
are here! No one will bring us back from
death to enjoy life after we die.*

ECCLESIASTES 3:22

KING SOLOMON'S WRITINGS IN ECCLESIASTES
read like the journal entries of a man on a
voyage of discovery. He observes and comments on the human condition: life; death;
the futility of pleasure; the importance of
wisdom, work, and fearing God.

He rhetorically questions the value of
work, contemplates human endeavor in connection with the various kinds of work God
has given people to do, and concludes that
"there is nothing better than to be happy and
enjoy ourselves as long as we can. And people should eat and drink and enjoy the fruits
of their labor, for these are gifts from God"
(Ecclesiastes 3:12-13).

Ralph Kozak's painting *Jesus Laughing*
hangs on the wall just above my desk. The

artist shows Jesus with head back and teeth gleaming, engaged in a fullmouthed laugh. You just know Jesus is enjoying the moment. The painting is a great reminder to me of the abundant life Jesus brings.

Sarah was nearly one hundred years old when Isaac was born. She had wanted nothing more than to give her husband a son, and when God granted her desire, Sarah exclaimed, "God has brought me laughter. All who hear about this will laugh with me" (see Genesis 21:1-6).

You needn't look too far in Scripture to find examples of God's proclivity for making people smile. When Nehemiah called for a celebration to mark Ezra's reading of the Torah, he insisted that the people share gifts of food with those who had nothing prepared (see Nehemiah 8:10). All through the Old Testament, he encouraged the Hebrews to celebrate. There's ample evidence that God wants his people to laugh and sing.

THERE'S AMPLE EVIDENCE THAT GOD WANTS HIS PEOPLE TO LAUGH AND SING.

LEADERS LEAD

At the time I wrote this chapter, a quick search on Google turned up 434,000 listings for the phrase *corporate fun and games*. All of the entries on the first couple of pages linked to consulting firms who help companies inject some hilarity into corporate meetings.

Another search, this time for the phrases *vice president of fun and games* and *director of fun and games* turned up nothing. It looks as if companies see a need for occasionally giving their people something to laugh about but none are willing to make it a full-time commitment.

I am only partially teasing.

Dozens of studies have proved that people who laugh at work are more productive. Laughter reduces stress, elevates endorphin levels, and helps to break monotony. It's easier to relate to people with whom you've shared a good laugh. If you like the people with whom you work, you will naturally feel better about your job. It's reasonable to draw corollaries between workplace laughter and improved performance.

Annual picnics and holiday gatherings are falling under the ax a bit more often these days as corporate budget managers look for ways to trim costs. If the evidence in favor of workplace fun is valid, in the long run these cuts will cost more than they save.

There are ways to make work more enjoyable with little or no added expense. One of my clients has a "Fun Committee" that looks for simple opportunities to add a smile. They organize events such as Crazy Shirt Day,

photo caption contests, and—my favorite—
Bring-Your-Favorite-Junk-Food Day.

I've heard of companies who have widened
the smiles of workers by relaxing restrictions
on what employees can use to decorate their
cubicles, and I was in an office just this week
where more than one person proudly told me
the rules had changed and that "now, every
day is jeans day."

LEADERSHIP RE:VISION

Pay close attention to the ending punctuation
of Genesis 4:1: "Adam had sexual relations
with his wife, Eve, and she became pregnant.
When she gave birth to Cain, she said, 'With
the LORD's help, I have produced a man!'"

Do you see the exclamation point? Eve was
excited. God had helped her do something
incredible. Unlike the creation of Adam and
Eve, which was God's work alone, he had allowed both of them, and Eve especially, to be
part of the wonder of Cain's birth.

God's gift to Eve gave her great joy.

One leadership attribute that's in short supply is the ability or desire to add joyful exclamation points to people's lives. Leaders who
themselves are overworked and racing along
a razor's edge of stress often do just the opposite. Instead of taking time to offer a chance
for laughter, they cultivate seeds of despair
and discontent.

As budgets tighten and profits decrease, I hear managers making statements to the effect that employees should be happy just to have jobs, and similar distressing comments. Can you imagine God being pleased with such talk? It's during tough economic times that workers need the

ADD JOYFUL
EXCLAMATION
POINTS TO
PEOPLE'S LIVES.

most encouragement. Instead, they often receive the greatest *dis*couragement.

God has promised you an abundant life, and he wants you to act as his agent in offering the same to those he's given you to lead. There's no way his plan for your staff includes a workplace that leaves them emotionally drained at day's end.

There's no easy fix, but that doesn't make it impossible. Nor does the difficulty excuse the need for you to seek a solution. Scripture says God honors those who diligently seek his truth, so let me encourage you to start the process.

Let the idea of being a loving shepherd roll around in your mind and heart for a few days, and see where it leads you. Find time to visit informally with a trusted member of your hourly staff, and ask for his or her candid opinion of the team's level of workplace joy.

Then ask God to help you see opportunities to add exclamation points.

27

IT'S NOT YOUR STUFF ANYWAY

David said, "No, my brothers! Don't be selfish with what the LORD has given us. He has kept us safe and helped us defeat the band of raiders that attacked us. Who will listen when you talk like this? We share and share alike—those who go to battle and those who guard the equipment."

1 SAMUEL 30:23-24

DAVID AND HIS ARMY HAD JUST DESTROYED the Amalekites. It had been a long, difficult battle. About two hundred of the men had been too exhausted to make the final push. Samuel's account says these men stayed behind.

The Israelites collected a vast amount of plunder in the battle, and when it came time to divide it up, a group of what Samuel refers to as "troublemakers" approached David demanding that those who didn't fight be denied any portion of the reward: "They didn't go with us, so they can't have any of the plunder we recovered" (1 Samuel 30:22).

David disagrees because he knows the

victory and the resulting treasure were gifts from God and that the plunder was actually God's to divide as he saw fit.

David was not being overgenerous. He was recognizing that everything he had came from God and would always be God's—to give and take as he desired.

Generosity is a common theme in Scripture. Consider the widow who caught the attention of Jesus by giving all she had, and remember the counsel of Paul to the wealthy, that "they should be rich in good works and generous to those in need, always being ready to share with others" (1 Timothy 6:18).

The Old Testament concept of Jubilee, in which debts are forgiven after a certain length of time, flies in the face of today's conventional wisdom, but if all provision comes from God and he wants to wipe the slate clean, who are we to stop him? It's not our stuff anyway.

LEADERS LEAD

I have worked with many advertising agencies in the course of my career, and all of them in one way or another go to great lengths to assure their clients that they will treat the clients' money *as if it were their very own*.

The sentiment is sincere, and I'm sure the ad agencies mean well, but wouldn't the clients be more comfortable with a promise that the agent would treat their money as if it *belonged to the clients*? Agents operate under the authority of their clients. They do what the clients direct. It's not the agents' money. It's the clients'.

It's not your stuff; it belongs to God.

Generosity extends beyond financial matters. Paul concludes a powerful treatise on mercy by reminding us that "everything comes from [God] and exists by his power and is intended for his glory" (Romans 11:36). If everything comes from God, and if everything exists for the purpose of bringing him glory, then nothing we have is ours. It's all his.

Think of all the things we call our own: our time, our possessions, our thoughts, our plans, our friends, our favorite pair of shoes, our past, our future, our faults, our talents. But none of that stuff really belongs to us. Nothing we have or lay claim to belongs to us. God allows us to manage it—on his behalf.

So, if all this stuff actually belongs to God and he has chosen you to act as his agent, what are you supposed to do with all of it? Your leadership abilities are a gift from God. He is counting on you to manage the resources he's provided in a way that's consistent with his character. And that's where the concept of generosity comes into full play.

YOUR LEADERSHIP ABILITIES ARE A GIFT FROM GOD.

As God's leadership agent, how do you stack up? Are you representing his generosity to those he's given you to lead?

When you evaluate your wage-and-benefit budgets, is your approach to give your employees as much as you can afford or as little as they'll accept?

When you offer people jobs, do you "go in low" to see if they'll take less than you are actually willing or able to pay? If they accept, have you tricked them into taking less than they're worth to you?

Do workers receive bonus packages proportional to those given executives? When it comes to profit sharing, do you share and share alike?

> ARE YOU REPRE-
> SENTING GOD'S
> GENEROSITY TO
> THOSE HE'S GIVEN
> YOU TO LEAD?

In your dealings with vendors, do you squeeze them past the point of reasonable requests in your negotiations for lower prices? Or do you generously work with them to find a mutually beneficial price and margin?

How generous are you with your time? Do you give enough of it to those who need it? Does your staff get enough time with you to fully understand what you want them to do, or does your schedule force them to guess at your priorities?

Do you cut people slack when they make mistakes? Do you allow room for error? God's mercy is magnanimous. Is yours? Are you generous with your forgiveness?

Real generosity doesn't wait to be asked. God loved you before you knew he existed. He provided for you before you felt the need. As a leader representing his interests, are your eyes roaming the landscape, looking for someone to bless with unexpected generosity?

28

DON'T SELL YOUR PRIORITIES FOR A BOWL OF SOUP

I have learned how to be content with whatever I have. I know how to live on almost nothing or with everything. I have learned the secret of living in every situation, whether it is with a full stomach or empty, with plenty or little. For I can do everything through Christ, who gives me strength.

PHILIPPIANS 4:11-13

LEADERSHIP OFTEN INVOLVES LEAVING THE security of your sheltered cove and venturing into unknown territory. Taking organizations to places they've never been requires leaders to weather storms of doubt, criticism, and the possibility of failure—public failure.

There are times when it seems as if people are standing in the wings, just waiting for you to trip and fall. They hate change so deeply that they'd rather sit in the dark dungeon of tired ideas than take a chance with the possibility of something new.

Paul was leading people to a place they'd

never been. Christianity was a completely new concept. Paul was blazing new trails physically and spiritually, and his was seldom a life of comfort. He lived in dire conditions and faced personal hatred wherever he went.

But through it all, Paul was sustained by the priorities he clung to. He had fixed his mind on the ultimate goal, and he used it as an anchor against the storms.

Job's wife told her husband to "curse God and die" when everything had turned against him. But his priority was to obey God, and nothing would dissuade him (see Job 2:9-10).

When Jesus was criticized for dining with corrupt government representatives and sinners, he clearly stated that his priorities did not include those who thought they were righteous (see Mark 2:15-17).

God knew Joshua would face doubt and uncertainty as he led the people into Canaan, and he helped Joshua set priorities by commanding him to "study this Book of Instruction continually. Meditate on it day and night so you will be sure to obey everything written in it" (Joshua 1:8).

LEADERS LEAD

Every organization is built on a set of values or priorities. Apple is known for the innovation of its personal-computing and electronic products. Ritz-Carlton has legendary customer-service standards. Maytag is dependable to the point where the poor repairman has become famous for having nothing to do. Southwest stands for low airfares.

In these and many other examples, it's the unwavering dedication to established priorities that have carved companies' brands into the common vernacular. These companies enjoy their leadership positions in the market because they have a good product or idea and stick with it no matter what.

Apple is often criticized for not allowing its superior operating system to run on any computer other than one manufactured by Apple itself. You can run Windows on a Mac, but you can't run OSX (the Mac Operating System) on anything but an Apple. The decision has undoubtedly cost Apple some market share, but the result has been a computing platform far more stable and reliable than that suffered by PC users. (You can probably guess I use a Mac.)

My point is not to start a PC-versus-Mac war but rather to emphasize the value of setting priorities and sticking with them. Southwest Airlines could probably gain a few new customers by serving meals, but doing so would force them to raise fares, which would jeopardize their position as a leader in offering low-priced air travel.

Just as there are examples of success attributed to strict adherence to priorities, there are also stories of great failures that resulted from people getting their priorities out of kilter. King Saul is probably the best biblical example of someone who had it all and then lost it all by compromising his values.

There are plenty of modern-day examples. You can probably name a few, tragic stories where individuals or organizations changed priorities to counter market demands and went downhill—fast. Esau was just the first in a long line of those who would squander a great future for the expedient pleasure of a bowl of soup.

LEADERSHIP RE:VISION

Having a set of solid priorities and values provides the perfect platform for effecting real change in your organization. You shouldn't change anything until you've decided what *isn't* going to change.

ESAU SQUANDERED A GREAT FUTURE FOR THE EXPEDIENT PLEASURE OF A BOWL OF SOUP.

When carpenters start to remodel a home, they first determine which of the walls they can't remove. Once they've identified the load-bearing walls, everything else can go, and the house will still stand, because what is left are the essential walls, similar to your company's or organization's core values or priorities.

In my consulting practice, I help leaders find new ways to do things, and the first step in any corporate renovation project is to determine the organization's load-bearing walls—the nonnegotiables. You'll get a much higher level of buy-in and support to a change initiative if everyone involved understands what *won't* change as a result.

But heed this warning: Sacred cows are not priorities.

SACRED COWS ARE NOT PRIORITIES.

Peter had been clinging to sacred cows and traditions when a transforming event changed his perspective. Peter experienced a vision:

> He saw the sky open, and something like a large sheet was let down by its four corners. In the sheet were all sorts of animals, reptiles, and birds. Then a voice said to him, "Get up, Peter; kill and eat them."
>
> "No, Lord," Peter declared. "I have never eaten anything that our Jewish laws have declared impure and unclean."
>
> But the voice spoke again: "Do not call something unclean if God has made it clean." (Acts 10:11-15)

Immediately after the vision, Peter leads a large group of Gentiles to Christ, and the young church begins to grow even faster. The vision hadn't changed Peter's priorities, just his perspective. What he had thought were nonnegotiables were hampering his real priority, which was sharing the gospel.

Have you allowed sacred cows or conventional wisdom to cloud your true priorities?

29

SOAR ON YOUR OWN WINGS

*He gives power to the weak and strength
to the powerless. Even youths will become
weak and tired, and young men will fall in
exhaustion. But those who trust in the LORD
will find new strength. They will soar high
on wings like eagles. They will run and not
grow weary. They will walk and not faint.*

ISAIAH 40:29-31

IN ROMANS 12:6, PAUL'S EXPOSITION ON PER-
sonal responsibilities, he reminds the Christians in Rome that God has given each of us
"different gifts for doing certain things well."
He reasons that God has given us these abilities with the expectation that we will put
them to good use. Those with teaching skills
should teach. Those good at serving should
serve. And those who've been blessed with
the ability to lead should "take the responsibility seriously" (Romans 12:8).

When it was time to build the first Tabernacle, God chose Bezalel to superintend the
massive project. To equip him for the task,

God filled Bezalel with "great wisdom, ability, and expertise in all kinds of crafts" (Exodus 31:3). Moses writes that Bezalel was a master at every craft.

Bezalel took charge. He used his talents to build a structure that was by all accounts intricate and immensely complex in its design. It's also important to note that Bezalel did the work. He was filled with the Spirit of God, but it was Bezalel himself and a host of other men and women who picked up the tools and physically built the Tabernacle.

The God who created everything from nothing stepped aside and gave Bezalel the task of building something because he knows that human beings derive pleasure from accomplishment. We enjoy doing what we do best. And I imagine God finds joy in watching us effectively use for his glory the skills he's given us.

LEADERS LEAD

People who are good at what they do are fun to watch. Athletes and musicians come to mind first. A few years ago there was a young man on our local high school football squad who could kick field goals like there was no tomorrow. The team as a whole wasn't very good, but if they could get inside his considerable range, they were all but guaranteed a score. Watching from the stands, you could sense that this player was totally in his element out there on the field.

My wife and I have season tickets to our local symphony, where we sit in the second row. From that up-close-and-personal vantage point we're able to see the eyes of guest soloists who perform with the orchestra. There are a handful who clearly love what they do. You can see in their eyes that they couldn't imagine ever doing anything else.

Effective leaders help people work with their strengths. The football coach didn't require his kicker to also play another position. He saw talent and helped the student develop it into a strength. World-class musicians may be able to play a variety of instruments because of their training, but they are seldom great at more than one. Focusing on your strengths can be a bit limiting on one hand, but doing so frees you to excel at something you enjoy doing.

> FOCUSING ON YOUR STRENGTHS FREES YOU TO EXCEL AT SOMETHING YOU ENJOY DOING.

Have you ever noticed that your fatigue threshold is much higher when you're doing something you love? We talk about being in one's zone or groove, and this must have something to do with a connection between our activity and the talents God has planted in each of us. We honor him by using the talents he's given us, and that makes us feel good.

LEADERSHIP RE:VISION

> *Those who trust in the LORD will find new strength. They will soar high on wings like eagles.*
>
> ISAIAH 40:31

Isaiah paints a powerful mental image with his promise of renewed strength for those who "trust in the LORD." The idea of God swooping down like an eagle and lifting you high above the clutter when you're weary is comforting, but it's not accurate.

Read the verse above again. God promises to give *you* new strength. He wants *you* to soar on wings like eagles. God is not picking you up and carrying you across the finish line. You are still running the race on your own two feet. And this is great news!

If you're like most good leaders with whom I'm familiar, you aren't looking for an easy way out. You'd rather stand on your own feet—or soar on your own wings—than allow someone else to carry the ball you've been handed. Like Bezalel, you want to build the Tabernacle, not stand by while someone else does it for you.

That's perfectly okay with God. All things

come from God, including your abilities. He's gifted you with certain strengths and wants you to "make the most of every opportunity," as Paul wrote in Colossians 4:5.

He has plans for you. Plans to do you good, not harm. That means he doesn't want to see you weary. It's not part of God's intent for people to be pushed until they burn out.

He wants to give you strength so that you can use the abilities he has given you for his glory.

> BURNOUT IS NOT PART OF GOD'S INTENT FOR ANYONE.

Great athletes understand the role proper nutrition plays in peak performance, and Jesus explained, "My nourishment comes from doing the will of God" (John 4:34). Doing God's will means waiting for him and following his lead. Isaiah promises that "those who trust in the LORD" will receive the nourishment they need to renew their strength.

Seek God's will. Make good use of the abilities he's given you. And you will soar on wings like eagles.

30

THE FINAL CHALLENGE

Don't copy the behavior and customs of this world, but let God transform you into a new person by changing the way you think.

ROMANS 12:2

THE PREVIOUS TWENTY-NINE CHAPTERS HAVE been about doing things differently, changing your habits, altering your behavior patterns from the ways of conventional wisdom through what I call a Leadership RE:Vision.

I've encouraged you to treat your employees and suppliers with a higher level of respect. You've been urged to push away from the table and curb your appetite for more and more and more.

I've asked you to revise the way you set wages, handle your PR, and manage your time as well as the time of those who follow your lead.

I hope you've seen some areas in your current leadership style that could benefit from RE:Vision, and I hope that you've made some commitments to actually do something about it.

But real Leadership RE:Vision is more about how you think than how you act.

Jesus knew that changing someone's behavior was impossible without changing his or her heart. The new covenant he introduced was based not on a set of rules but on a change of heart. The abundant life he came to give was more metaphysical than temporal.

Meeting Jesus changed people's lives, but more important, it changed their hearts and minds.

So the final chapter in this little book about seeing leadership through a new set of lenses is a challenge. It asks a critically important question—What has God changed your mind about lately?—and then helps you determine the answer for yourself.

RENEWING YOUR MIND

What has God changed your mind about lately?

Don't answer too quickly. It's a bigger question than you think. There's a temptation to fire off an answer as if to prove you have an open mind. No one wants to be accused of being small-minded. So it's easy to rattle off something about listening to new types of music or reading fiction while on vacation. But I'm talking about substantive change. Real change. Life-changing change.

If God is going to take the time to change your mind about something, the change is bound to be significant. When God steps into your life to craft a new perspective for you, you can bet your last buck it will transcend the type of music used in Sunday worship services. It will go beyond the choice of a Bible translation, and it'll reach past the style of clothing people wear or the amount of metal they have stuck in their eyebrows.

IF GOD IS GOING TO TAKE THE TIME TO CHANGE YOUR MIND ABOUT SOMETHING, THE CHANGE IS BOUND TO BE SIGNIFICANT.

Perhaps I should rephrase the question to represent a change of heart, or a change of attitude, as in, Where has God's Spirit been working to change your attitude lately?

Will there be a test? If books had final exams, the essay question at the end of this chapter would be, "Tell me, in 250 words or less, how God has changed your mind lately."

The prompt would continue: "Don't go overboard with unnecessary explanations and fluff. Just tell me where you were, where you are now, and what God did to bring you to the new perspective."

A DIVINE
CONTRADICTION

God is something of a paradox, isn't he?

We are told from an early age that God is the same yesterday, today, and forever. That's one of the things I find most attractive about God. He is the one constant in my life, the one thing I know will never change. I've been lashed to the mast of storm-tossed ships and saved from drowning many times by heeding the advice of Hebrews 12:2 to look above the clutter and keep my eyes on Jesus.

We sing a hymn that describes God being "from age to age the same." He's the beginning and the end. The first word and the final word.

Solid rock. A shelter in the time of storm.

The great hymn "Holy, Holy, Holy" describes God as someone "which wert and art and evermore shall be."

Now here's where the paradox comes into play: God is also a God of change.

Scripture is full of stories relating to God's creativity, to his penchant for doing things that have never been done before. He is a God of new ideas.

From the very beginning we see God doing new things. The first page of his book sets the stage for an eternity of change. The first lesson he teaches us is that he doesn't put much stock in status quo. Keeping things as they are is not what God is all about.

In the beginning, darkness was the norm. It wasn't that things weren't light. They had always been dark; there had never been anything but darkness. There wasn't an absence of light, because there had never been any light to be absent. You can't miss what you've never had. The universe had never seen light. Darkness was the only thing there had ever been.

God stepped into that darkness, or was already there and evidenced himself into that, and did what? He changed things. He created light. He did something that had never been done before.

ETERNALLY FAITHFUL. TOTALLY UNPREDICTABLE.

It wasn't more of the same only better, which is what we do a lot of times, isn't it?

If stuff isn't going well at work or with our families or with some other aspect of our lives, we just apply more of the same. We do the same thing only bigger, faster, stronger, harder, louder, longer, or with more variety.

If I can't get things done at work, I take a time-management course so I have one more thing not to get done. We are all guilty of that. Albert Einstein actually wrote once that the definition of insanity is doing the same thing over and over and expecting a different result.

At the very beginning of God's book, we see that he isn't satisfied with letting things stand. "Let there be light" was a completely new concept. It had never been done before.

NEW HOME. NEW JOB. NEW NAME.

A couple of pages further along in Genesis, we come across a fellow named Abram, who lived with his father, Terah, in a place called Ur of the Chaldeans.

When I was a kid that was my favorite town, Ur of the Chaldeans. I still love to say it.

"Where are you going on vacation?"

"We found this amazing Internet site for a resort in Urrrrrrrr of the Chaldeeeeeans."

Later, after Terah had already moved his family to Haran, some six hundred miles from Ur, and settled there, God picked up Abram and moved him: "Leave your native country, your relatives, and your father's family, and go to the land that I will show you" (Genesis 12:1).

Leaving the place you were born to live in a new place is not unusual for us these days. How many people do you know who live near the town in which they were born? I did a quick survey once while leading a men's retreat. Of the one hundred guys in the room, only two of them lived in or near the town of their birth.

The U.S. Census Bureau says that about 15 percent of us move to new addresses every year, but in the time of Terah and Abram, a move to a new place was extremely rare. People just didn't do things like that. You lived where you lived. You were born, you lived, and you died—in the same place.

God's asking Abram to move was not like asking us to move. Understand what a huge change this was for Abram. This was something that typically wasn't done.

If you listen carefully, you can hear the people around Haran mumbling to one another: "Did you hear about that crazy Abram? He says he is going to leave here and travel to a new place!"

Don't forget, this was thousands of years ago. The Internet hadn't been invented. There was no Google and no Orbitz. Abram was going where no one he knew had ever been. And it was much more than just relocation. God wanted to start a whole new race of people with Abram: new nation, new religion, new everything. Once again, God proves he is a God of change by doing something that completely and unmistakably destroys the status quo. It's critical to note that he didn't do it with incremental changes. He didn't tell Abram to stay in Ur of the Chaldeans or Haran so he could make some minor adjustments in Abram's life, which would eventually result in a new nation of people outnumbering the stars of the heavens. We don't hear God telling Abram to make some minor adjustments to see how things work out. The message couldn't have been any clearer: Leave and go someplace new.

And it was more than just a physical move. Abram's entire perspective on deity changed. As a Chaldean, Abram had been brought up as a polytheist. He had been taught to worship many gods, and now he was being told by one of them that his religion was going to be singular, that he was going to follow Yahweh, and only Yahweh.

Abram was no longer in his father's land; he was no longer "his father's son." He no longer did what his father did. Are you in the same profession your dad is in or was in?

Finally, God changed Abram's personal identity by giving him a new name. As children, one of the first questions we learn to answer is, What's your name? Once we learn it, it doesn't usually change.

Do you know anyone whose first name is different from the one he or she was born with? If so, that person is probably the exception to the rule.

God is a God of change.

Reggie McNeil writes and speaks about dramatic changes happening in the church. At a conference he led in 2005, Reggie spoke about what he calls "Red Sea moments." As he put it, God is forever finding unique ways to solve problems.

Examine the record of God's interaction with humanity. In story after story, we are presented with a God who would rather invent a new solution than go with something that's been done before.

Consider these:

- Are you hungry? Okay, I'll drop manna from heaven.
- Need to cross the Jordan River at flood stage? I'll cause an earthquake that will block the river.
- Five thousand hungry people to feed? Where's that boy with the lunch box?

The last one is one of my favorites. Thousands of people to feed, and the disciples do what most of us would do. They turn to their tried-and-proven list of sensible solutions and suggest to Jesus that he send the people home: "Isn't there a McMutton's back there by the camel stop?"

But that wouldn't work for a God who's all

about change. Anyone can do what's expected. No one would have been surprised if Jesus had said, "Well folks, it's late, and I know you're getting hungry. I'm going to wrap it up so you can head for home while the light is still good."

But God does the unexpected more often than not.

YOU CAN'T LEAD WITH OLD IDEAS

Leading means going places you haven't been and doing things no one else has done. Leaders boldly go where no one has gone before. Managing involves staying where you are and making things work.

Leading means taking your group, yourself, whatever it is you're to lead, to new places.

> LEADING MEANS GOING PLACES YOU HAVEN'T BEEN AND DOING THINGS NO ONE ELSE HAS DONE.

Reggie McNeil suggests looking for Red Sea moments before rolling out the old boat and floating across the water.

God is a God of new ideas.

I'm sure you are familiar with these statements from Lamentations 3:22-23:

- "The faithful love of the LORD never ends!" Constant.

- "His mercies never cease." Constant.
- "Great is his faithfulness." Constant.
- "His mercies begin afresh each morning." *Paradox*.

God's mercies are *new* every morning. This unchanging, always faithful, unceasingly steady God provides new mercies every morning.

Why? Because he created us. He wrote the owner's manual. He knows we get bored. He knows we get distracted. He knows we get set in our ways.

He knows we get our theologies figured out and locked in place. He gave us minds to think and reason and process new things, and he knows we tend to get lazy and stop using them. So, to keep us excited about his ever-changing mercies, he changes them daily.

The sunrise is different every morning. The birds chirping are different every morning. He brings new people into our lives, each one with different ideas, perspectives, and solutions. I don't particularly like new people because they take some getting used to and they're *different*. But life would be excruciatingly dull without them. God changes me because he loves me.

Change isn't always easy. New shoes don't fit as nicely as the old ratty ones. New songs have words I need to memorize. New people bring diversity, and diversity is difficult because some of those new people say things I don't agree with or do things I think they shouldn't. Even worse, they tell me that I need to change the way I think about things I already have figured out and locked in. All of which proves God's love for me, because he knows how bored I would get if nothing ever changed.

CHANGING YOUR MIND CAN GLORIFY GOD

God is a God of new ideas. And he wants us to entertain new ideas. Throughout the Scriptures we see him introducing new ideas into humanity, into history. The evidence in favor of change is overwhelming. God wants us to entertain new ideas.

A willingness to entertain new ideas is critical to our spiritual health.

Think about the Pharisees. In every movie about Easter, from *Jesus Christ Superstar* to *The Passion of the Christ*, we saw the Pharisees depicted as really bad guys. The pictures in our little Sunday school lessons showed the Pharisees wearing black robes. In Easter pageants, no one wanted to play the part of a Pharisee because they were evil. Right?

Well, I don't know if they were all that bad.

Consider this: These men in black were

doing what they believed God wanted them to do. They were living up to a standard they were certain God had established. They were thinking exactly what they thought God wanted them to think.

The problem is, they hadn't considered a new idea in hundreds of years. They had blinders on. Generations of following God in a never-changing manner had blinded them to God's ability to bring "new mercies" into their lives. God's creativity was all around them, and they refused to acknowledge it.

So what did God do?

> In the sixth month of Elizabeth's pregnancy, God sent the angel Gabriel to Nazareth, a village in Galilee, to a virgin named Mary. She was engaged to be married to a man named Joseph, a descendant of King David. Gabriel appeared to her and said, "Greetings, favored woman! The Lord is with you!"
> Confused and disturbed, Mary tried to think what the angel could mean. (Luke 1:26-29)

The angel's words to Mary definitely didn't fit into her framework of conventional wisdom.

> "Don't be afraid, Mary," the angel told her, "for you have found favor with God!" (1:30)

Now that statement is strange all by itself, because the status quo didn't really allow for women to have *any* status with God, let alone favor.

> "You will conceive and give birth to
> a son, and you will name him Jesus.
> He will be very great and will be
> called the Son of the Most High. The
> Lord God will give him the throne of
> his ancestor David. And he will reign
> over Israel forever; his Kingdom will
> never end!"
> Mary asked the angel, "But how can
> this happen? I am a virgin." (1:31-34)

Think about it: No virgin had ever conceived a child. In fact, the way God designed procreation involves a woman's losing her virginity. Children don't come any other way.

But this Child and his birth would be like no other. So God "broke his own rules."

He stepped into history and did something that had never been done before, and we get another example of a Red Sea moment.

NEW SOLUTIONS FOR NEW SITUATIONS

God packs his book with stories of unique solutions because he wants us to look beyond our conventional wisdom for answers. He doesn't want us to rely on our own understanding but instead look to him for fresh perspectives.

In the tenth chapter of Joshua, we read how the Hebrew army was up against the Amorites, who had an army much bigger than Joshua's. Scripture doesn't say for certain, but you can imagine the discussion going on in Joshua's tent the night before the battle.

The Hebrew generals would no doubt have been running through the options they saw based on past experience. Perhaps scouts had come back with reports on where the Amorites might be most vulnerable. The generals may have been drawing up plans for an ambush or a surprise attack. One or two generals may even have suggested the possibility of surrender and negotiation.

Here's what really happened:

> Joshua traveled all night from Gilgal and took the Amorite armies by surprise. The LORD threw them into a panic, and the Israelites slaughtered great numbers of them at Gibeon. . . . As the Amorites retreated down the road from Beth-horon, the LORD destroyed them *with a terrible hailstorm* from heaven that continued until they reached Azekah. The hail killed

more of the enemy than the Israelites killed with the sword. (Joshua 10:9-11, emphasis added)

I'm pretty sure we can rule out "Let's have a hailstorm!" as one of the possible strategies Joshua's generals would have suggested. It wasn't simply a crazy idea; it had never been done before, and the possibility of making it happen was completely outside of their control. Until that time, no one had ever depended on the weather to take out an enemy. But God is a God of new ideas.

So here's that question again: *What has God changed your mind about lately?*

What old ideas are you carrying around that need to be dusted off and renovated? Are there areas of your behavior, your attitude, or your perspective that would sound familiar to the Pharisees? Are you holding on to ideas and attitudes because they've worked in the past or are comfortable? Are some of those ideas locked away in your mind behind a door to which you haven't given God the key? Of course, God is omnipresent, and he can go anywhere he chooses. But there are areas in our lives over which God doesn't have control because he has given each of us the freedom of choice—it's called free will. We hold the keys to some of those doors in our minds and in our hearts.

Do you have some things that you need to open up so God can dust them off? What if God has a Red Sea moment with your name on it?

Let's go back to the place where this whole idea started.

Moses is standing at the edge of the Red Sea, and there are perhaps a couple million tired, cranky, and frightened people behind him. Within their recent past they had seen God take care of the Egyptians in some rather incredible ways—frogs, boils, locusts, death of the firstborn. They probably thought God was going to rain some awesome terror from the sky and wipe Pharaoh off the face of the earth. They may even have been praying for another plague.

Instead, we see another in the eternal series of Red Sea solutions from our amazing and infinitely creative God: "Moses raised his hand over the sea, and the LORD opened up a path through the water with a strong east wind. The wind blew all that night, turning the seabed into dry land. So the people of Israel walked through the middle of the sea on dry ground, with walls of water on each side!" (Exodus 14:21-22).

What if God has a Red Sea moment waiting for you?

I heard recently of a church in California that raised millions of dollars for mission work in the community by selling their building and meeting in a rented facility. Talk about a Red Sea solution!

God told Moses to do something completely different, and look what happened as a result. What if Moses had argued with God or tried to do something that fit nicely into his basket of conventional wisdom?

What has God changed your mind about lately?

Perhaps your response to that question should be a prayer something like this: "Lord, show me where you want me to change my mind."

What would happen if you prayed for some Red Sea moments?

SCRIPTURE INDEX

TOPICAL INDEX

AUTHOR'S NOTE

I love writing books because the process forces me to
focus my thinking on a specific topic and explore ideas
to greater depths than I normally would. This concept
of revising one's leadership perspectives has been a
learning experience for me. I haven't practiced to
perfection every piece of advice in this book, and I
probably never will. My claim is not one of "expert
leader" but rather one of "willing conduit" for fresh
ways of thinking and looking at the status quo.

The two people who know more about my shortcomings than anyone else are my wife, Rhonda, and
daughter, Noelle. They'll read these pages and wonder
why I can't live up to the ideal, but they'll continue to
forgive and to exhibit incredible patience with me.
Writing a book is especially difficult on them because
I am frequently "away," either literally or figuratively,
during the process.

My friend and agent, Mark Sweeney, is the iron
that sharpens my dull blade. Jon Farrar and Ron
Beers at Tyndale gave me the freedom I needed to
catch and share the ideas. Sue Taylor made the words
sound so much better. Kathy McClelland helped get
the word out.

Writing, for me, is a lonely profession, but there are
a few who came alongside with suggestions, ideas, and
support. Joe Brown, Andy Butcher, and John Seybert
helped me get unstuck in a couple of places. Dana
Ostby offered encouragement at exactly the right time.
Bob Turner, Nigel Whitehead, Brian Farone, and a host
of others never showed any signs of fatigue when I
launched into a too-long recitation of my struggles
with the manuscript. I need to acknowledge the vital
role these folks played in the completion of this work.

And to the One who took great care in knitting me

together in my mother's womb, thank you for giving me the ability to string words along in such a fashion as will compel others to learn from what I've observed. I occasionally catch a glimpse of your plan to do me good, and I am amazed at the way you love me.

Jim Seybert
August 2008
Arroyo Grande, California

ABOUT THE AUTHOR

Jim Seybert has worked with leaders of small and large organizations, helping them to think differently about what they do. His clients include entertainment and publishing giants, health-care providers, retailers, nonprofits, and real-estate developers.

In Jim's free time, he likes to take deep breaths along the High Sierra trails of Yosemite National Park. Jim and his wife live in California.

Look for these other
leadership books from
Tyndale House Publishers, Inc.

CP0282